MW01632168

25 LIES

EXPOSING DEMOCRATS' MOST DANGEROUS, SEDUCTIVE, DAMNABLE, DESTRUCTIVE LIES

AND HOW TO REFUTE THEM

25 LIES

EXPOSING DEMOCRATS' MOST DANGEROUS, SEDUCTIVE, DAMNABLE, DESTRUCTIVE LIES AND HOW TO REFUTE THEM

Vince Everett Ellison

BOMBARDIER BOOKS
An Imprint of Post Hill Press
ISBN: 978-1-63758-692-1
ISBN (eBook): 978-1-63758-248-0

25 Lies:
Exposing Democrats' Most Dangerous, Seductive, Damnable, Destructive Lies and How to Refute Them

Author Photo by Ella Ellison
Cover Photo by Erica Ellison
Cover Design by Tiffani Shea

Post Hill Press
New York • Nashville
posthillpress.com

Published in the United States of America
1 2 3 4 5 6 7 8 9 10

I dedicate this book to:

Jesus Christ

My wife and children
Ivory and Ella Wee Ellison
Dr. John and Chorsie Calhoun
Johanna Loeb

CONTENTS

INTRODUCTION

"The degree of civilization in a society can be judged by entering its prisons."

—Fyodor Dostoevsky

NOTHING IN MY LIFE had prepared me for what I was about to experience. I was only twenty-six years old and had placed myself in harm's way. I had voluntarily agreed to be locked in a cage with over one thousand criminals who wanted to kill me. I was to supervise 127 of them, mostly alone, for eight hours a day as a correctional officer at the Kirkland Correctional Institution in Columbia, South Carolina. It was the start of my postgraduate education.

I had graduated from the South Carolina Criminal Justice Academy, where I had been elected class president. "If you want to survive, you better forget all of the academy sh#t" was the first lesson I learned from officers and inmates alike. They were right.

When I first walked inside that prison, I was scared to death. This fear was a strange feeling because I was not afraid of conflict. I had been immersed in it my entire life while growing up in the hinterlands and backwoods of Haywood County, Tennessee, where your intelligence was prized second to your toughness. Sports and physical competition were a way of life. My brothers and I were raised among very tough, independent, and

GOD-fearing people. But we were also well-versed in how to recognize, avoid, and confront an enemy. Haywood County, Tennessee, had been Klan country in my youth. By the time I was an adult, the Black men, not the FBI, had run the Ku Klux Klan out of Haywood County. These men trained me.

Remnants of the Klan were there and recognizable, but we did not fear them. They feared us. I was taught never to fear these men, and I never have.

I believed my toughness had been proven after playing football in high school and college. I'd been involved in bits of roughhousing and a few serious fights in my youth. Nevertheless, nothing had prepared me for this intense experience.

In a prison, you don't just experience evil—you experience concentrated evil. At Kirkland, inmates were housed by classification through a given psychological profile. They were classified as either beta, meaning passive; gamma, meaning average; or alpha, meaning aggressive. My station post was dormitory B1, which housed the high alphas. Theses alpha inmates were the most violent and unpredictable in the prison. Why house all these violent inmates in the same dormitory? Prison officials believed that placed among the general prison population, alphas would victimize betas and gammas, but housed together, they'd cancel each other out. I, therefore, did not just experience concentrated evil daily. I experienced "extra-concentrated" evil daily. My job was to maintain security, custody, and control of unit B1.

Utterly intimidated during the first two days, I was afraid to conduct my rounds behind the wing gates where the inmates lived in the cells, and the inmates knew it. I was losing respect. I was losing control of the dormitory. My dorm keeper and trustee was a Nation of Islam Muslim named Elijah Muhammad II. After my second day, he decided to confront me regarding my passivity.

He said to me, "Officer Ellison, you are gonna have to decide whether you want to do this job. Tomorrow you are gonna have to come in and take control of this dorm, or you're gonna get hurt or killed." He pointed at my badge and said, "That badge doesn't just represent you. If one of these inmates bother you, that badge means every officer at this prison will stand with you. If that's not enough, add every officer in the state. If that's not enough, add every police officer. If that's not enough, add the Army, Navy, Air Force, and Marine Corps." He continued by saying, "It seems like everybody in this dorm knows that except you."

The next day I came to B1 on a mission. It was like the feeling I had right before covering the opening kickoff in a football game. I wanted to knock somebody's head off! I immediately got the chance.

I gave an inmate a direct order to move along and not loiter in the hallway. He was bigger than me and was an alpha. Of course, he refused, and I wanted him to refuse. I threw him down a flight of stairs, cuffed him, and threw him in his cell. I walked back upstairs and yelled, "EVERYBODY OUT OF THE M@#$F#K%$^N HALLWAY!!!" They all scattered. From that day until the day I left, I was the alpha.

This job in this prison taught me how to recognize and confront evil. Now I recognize it on sight. I was trained by the best people in law enforcement and by the best criminal minds. For hours a day, I looked into the eyes of vicious murderers, rapists, and drug kingpins. I closely observed them when they lied to me, when they tried to con me, when they tried to intimidate me, and when they wanted to kill me. I then had the opportunity to compare their visage with that of the average citizen, and the differences were striking. I've always had a discerning spirit, but the education at Kirkland elevated it.

Nevertheless, my official duties did not demand that I separate myself from all compassion and the need to understand. These men were guilty of aggravated murder, serial murder, serial rape, burglary, and selling drugs. More than anything, they were extraordinarily violent and enjoyed being violent. Dostoevsky said, "Nothing is easier to denounce than the evildoer; nothing is more difficult than to understand him." This prison soon became my social laboratory.

As I wrote in my previous book *The Iron Triangle*:

> Most of these young men were my age, gender, and race. Nevertheless, they were in jail, and I was not. Why? Thirty years after the Civil Rights Movement I believed that Black Americans had overcome. I was wrong. Blacks had lost ground. South Carolina had three prisons in 1980. It had thirty by 2000. I discovered three criteria that most of those young Black me had in common. 1) Fatherless Home. 2) No High School Diploma. 3) Lived in Poverty. These criminals were not born. They were made.

> Consequently, after almost fifty years, trillions of dollars, mammoth legislation, hundreds of marches, riots, and murder, nothing has changed… Many can argue that things have gotten worse. AIDS, incarceration, crime, or family breakdown was not an issue in 1963. But they are huge problems today.… A *Time* magazine article by Jack White in 1999 said Black men were an endangered species. The same article cites murder by another Black man as the number one cause of death between Black men aged fifteen to twenty-four… This is all planned. I can say this with some certainty because these apocalyptic statistics pre-

> dicting the destruction of Black America have been known for decades. The Heritage Foundation released statistics revealing that one in twelve or 8.5 percent of all Black men living in Washington, DC, will be murdered before their forty-fifth birthday.

I learned how to recognize evil in real time, to look behind the eyes. My very life depended on it. I excelled in that environment. I know evil. It devastated me when I saw this evil in the people of the clergy, civil rights, and politics that I admired.

The absence of a father's discipline. The assault on Christianity and Christian education. The corruption of the arts through music, movies, porn, and video games had created a generation of monsters.

But to what end? Power. These men were collateral damage in a war to subvert, monetize, and control the Black vote in the Black community. To win elections in America, Democrats need 90 percent of the Black vote. To accomplish this heresy, they must enslave Blacks again. Previously, Democrats employed the whip and the shackles. Today they use poverty, drugs, mass incarceration, failing schools, the perversion of morality, and the repression of religious liberties as their weapons.

I had been trained to recognize this evil in men. This evil is present in smaller portions throughout society. In the prisons, the concentration was higher. But I had begun to keep company with a group's leadership where there was an extraordinarily high concentration. This leadership's goal was the exploitation, not the betterment, of the people I was in charge of securing from society. I saw the same expressions of cruelty, avarice, and pride in their eyes. It was the leadership of the Democrat Party. I see it clearly in their visage, spirit, and action. I am annoyed and amazed that others do not.

But my opinion means nothing. I had to confirm my suspicions with the word of GOD. I was taught, "A righteous man is one who submits his will to the will of GOD." This definition alone identifies the Democrat Party as supremely unrighteous. Their leadership has their own Will and cares nothing for the Will of GOD. Their entire legislative agenda can be characterized by the acronym SEM (sex, envy, murder).

The Democrat Party's method of implanting self-hatred and division into its Black population has been so successful that their methods have been incorporated by tyrants worldwide. So despicable are these methods that children's cartoons display them in an attempt to warn against their cruelty. One such instance occurs in the Disney movie *The Hunchback of Notre Dame*. Seemingly taking his cue from over 200 years of Democrat Party oppression, Judge Claude Frollo convinced the good-natured hunchback, Quasimodo, to hate himself utilizing the methods Democrats have wielded to teach most Blacks to hate themselves for centuries. Through Critical Race Theory, this same Democrat Party is attempting to pass this same self-hatred to White children as well.

Like the poison of Democrat Hollywood porn and hip-hop music in Black Democrat culture, Judge Claude Frollo taught the hunchback to hate himself by corrupting the arts. Through music, he taught the hunchback a song that said the world hated him; he was deformed; he was ugly; he was a monster. He told the hunchback that he was his only friend, and he could only protect him if he obeyed and did not leave his sphere of influence; in this case it was the Notre Dame Cathedral. In the case of the Democrat Party, it is the inner city ghettoes. He made the hunchback recite this self-hating song, thus forcing his participation in his own destruction.

We learn through repetition. Through repetition, we learn habits. Habits create a culture. Democrats have created a culture of death. Democrats have spoken these death statements to Black America with such regularity that Blacks now recite them to themselves and teach them to their children. Consequently, Black Democrats rob, rape, assault, and murder each other in numbers that stagger the mind and are not comparable anywhere in the Western world. Amazingly, even though 99 percent of the Black inmates are victims and products of the Democrat Party system, like prisoners released from the communist gulags or Chinese reeducation camps, they remain faithful to the Democrat Party orthodoxy before and after release. Sadly, I am one of the very few who recognize this evil and am willing to confront it. Why? Rattlesnakes trained me to defend myself against rattlesnakes. I have lived with, controlled, and dominated Devils. As a child of GOD and an heir of Jesus Christ, I'm not afraid of a damn thing. The children of GOD no longer have policy disagreements with the Democrat Party leadership. These people are not misguided or ill-informed. My experiences have afforded me the unique ability to recognize evil at first glance.

For you who attempt to use the words of Jesus against me and try to defend abortion, religious repression, child exploitation, and racism by saying, "Who are you to judge?" I will remind you that the words of Jesus Christ can never be used to justify carnal actions. I will not remain silent in the presence of evil. Therefore, I say with clarity and absolution:

"The Democrat Party leadership is EVIL!!"

My goal is to warn and provide you with the information to deliver you from this evil.

I see the Democrats coming to kill, steal, and destroy. My hope is to help you see them.

PROLOGUE:

WHAT IS EVIL?

"The greatest trick the Devil ever pulled was convincing the world he didn't exist."

—Charles Baudelaire

"The second greatest trick the Devil ever pulled was convincing the world he is the good guy."

—Ken Ammi

"A brave man is a man who dares to look the Devil in the face and tells him he is a Devil."

—James A. Garfield, the twentieth US president

SINCE 1800, THE DEMOCRAT PARTY leadership has been the most perpetually evil organization on the face of this earth. For over 220 years they've supported slavery, promoted lynchings, instigated civil war, and commit infanticide through abortion. Because of the millions of kidnapped Blacks that died under Democrat Party captivity and the sixty million abortions conducted in Democrat-operated, -funded and -protected abortion clinics, I estimate that the Democrat Party, with its own hands, has killed over 100 million Americans (60 percent of them Black). They instituted a racist crime bill that imprisoned millions of Black fathers, destroying the Black family. The Democrat Party stole $58 trillion in property and labor from Black Americans, according to a July 7, 2019, article in OurTimePress.com by David Mark Greaves. Democrats lock poor children in failing schools and fail to protect citizens while disarming them in Democrat-controlled war zones. Democrats control every place in America where race hatred has looted and burned neighborhoods to the ground. They control every ghetto, every drug corner, every housing project, every failing school, and every abortion clinic in America. And finally, removing their masks, The Heritage Foundation reported that on February 18, 2021, all the Democrats in the House of Representatives voted to call the practice of Christianity discriminatory by passing "The Equality Act," placing the rights of LGBTQ (lesbian, gay, bisexual, transgender, queer) citizens over the teachings of Jesus Christ and over the religious liberties of Christians, Muslims, and Jews. This blasphemy is just a tiny example of the carnage Democrats have inflicted on the American people. Today's Democrat Party is an evil organization. If Satan walks on this earth, he lays his head at the DNC (Democratic National Committee). In this book, I will prove it.

In the movie *The Matrix*, a human being was reduced to nothing more than a battery, tolerated to serve the needs of the machines. To the Democrat Party the Black American has been reduced to nothing more than a vote, tolerated to serve the needs of the Democrat Party. This party has been very adroit at casting the weight of their sins on all of America. Even in Spike Lee's *Malcolm X* in the opening monologue, Denzel Washington, playing Malcolm X, mistakenly charged all White men with the sins of the Democrat Party. Republican White men passed the Thirteenth Amendment ending slavery, the Fourteenth Amendment providing equal protection and due process, the Fifteenth Amendment providing the vote to Black men, and the Nineteenth Amendment allowing the vote for all women—Black, White, and so forth—with very little Democrat support.

So, to correct the history, instead of charging the White man, Malcolm X's "I Have a Nightmare (I Charge the White Man)" speech in front of a Black audience should have gone like this:

> Brothers and sisters, I'm here to tell you that I charge the Democrat Party. I charge the Democrat Party with being the greatest murderer on earth. I charge the Democrat Party with being the greatest kidnapper on earth. There is no place in the world that that Party can go and say it created peace and harmony. Everywhere the Democrats have gone they've created destruction. So, I charge the Democrats. I charge the Democrats with being the greatest kidnapper on this earth. I charge the Democrats with being the greatest robber and enslaver on this earth. I charge the Democrats with being the greatest drunkards on this earth.
>
> They can't deny the charges. You can't deny the charges. We're the living proof of those charges. You and I are the proof...you and I, we've never seen any democracy. We ain't seen no democracy in the cotton fields of Georgia. That wasn't no democracy in there. We didn't see any democracy on the streets of Harlem and the streets of Brooklyn and the streets of

> Detroit and Chicago. That wasn't democracy down there. No, we've never seen democracy; all we've seen is hypocrisy. We don't see any American dream. We've experienced only the Democrat Party nightmare.

But who am I to say the Democrat Party is evil? No one. But I did not define them. Their actions illustrate their malevolence. Their callous disregard for human life is on display in the ghettoes of America, the citizens of Afghanistan, and all over the world. I am persuaded that most of the people who vote for and serve in the Democrat Party are people of goodwill. And are like Oskar Schindler in the movie *Schindler's List*, who became a Nazi for survival; or JoJo Betzler, in the film *JoJo Rabbit*, who became a Nazi from indoctrination. Likewise, many good Democrats are trapped in an evil, one-party system with the party leadership willing and able to destroy anyone who does not conform. The fact that most sane people could not imagine the extent of their evil protected the Nazi Party then and the Democrat Party now from the inspection and retaliation of the people.

Nevertheless, before evil can be defeated, it must first be confronted, defined, and called by its name. Jesus Christ defined the Pharisees and the Sadducees as evil. Slavery was defined as evil by Abraham Lincoln and Frederick Douglass. Nazism was defined as evil by Winston Churchill and Franklin D. Roosevelt. Ronald Reagan described the Soviet Union as an "Evil Empire." Terrorism was defined as evil by George W. Bush. And the Democrat Party leadership is defined as evil by the WORD OF GOD.

Thomas Jefferson said, "We are not afraid to follow truth wherever it may lead, nor to tolerate any error so long as reason is left free to combat it." Unable to defend their lies with reason through debate in the public square, evil Democrats, like the evil Nazis, have resorted to dictatorial powers against free speech. Cancel culture, censorship, boycotts, intimidation, riots, and murder are now accepted methods exercised by the Democrat Party to kill resistance. But this is nothing new. These hoodlum and gangster methods were exacted against the Black slaves, Catholics, the abolitionists, the sharecroppers, and the civil rights workers. Today, Democrats use these tactics against Christians, life activists, education freedom activists, pro-Second Amendment activists, and religious liberty activists. Understand, tyrants never bother with censuring a lie, for a lie will be proven false. Tyrants censure the truth because truth will destroy a tyrant.

From slavery and Jim Crow to abortion, the Democrat Party has spawned generations of leaders who were no more than a cabal of perverts, liars, and psychopaths. Settling scores, unleashing wanton destruction, and exacting revenge on America are the only reasons these victims are hell-bent on obtaining power. They embrace every law promoting murdering babies, abusing and exploiting illegal immigrants, restricting religious liberties, disarming citizens, confiscating wealth, incarcerating masses, expanding poverty, indoctrinating children, legalizing drugs, undermining science, and encouraging vice, while obstructing every effort to reign them in. Their actions are evil. Therefore, they are evil. *Their evil is compounded because they lie, and more so, they take such pride in their lies.* They are successful because they are prolific at instigating strife between the children of GOD. In this book, I will expose their lies and provide you with the tools to defeat them.

I wrote this book because I love everyone, which means I LOVE DEMOCRATS (and there's nothing they can do about it). In John 15:17 Jesus says, "These things I command you, that ye love one another." I have no choice. GOD has given the command. Even if they hate me, I will love them. I also love my country. Therefore, I must warn it about the evil plans of the Democrat Party.

In his "House Divided" speech in 1858, Abraham Lincoln warned America about the evil intent of the Democrat Party when he said: "I believe this government cannot endure, permanently half slave and half free.... It will become all one thing, or all the other." Lincoln knew then that the enslavement of all people, Black and White, was the Democrat Party leadership's primary objective; it remains their goal even today. The enslavement of poor and middle-class Americans under the heel of the Democrat Party elite then and now bear witness to this truth.

I have learned that whenever you find conflict among two people or two groups of people, you should always look for the third party. The third party is the instigator. They benefit from chaos and destruction. They are the snake in the garden; they are Iago in *Othello*; they are the yellow journalists who instead of saying "Police Officer Kills Unarmed American," they say, "White Policeman Kills Unarmed Black Man." The third party is the Democrat Party. They live on hatred, envy, and violence. Their primary goal is to inflame the hatred between Black and White, and Christians, causing a schism in the Body of Christ. We must identify the Democrat instigators and negate their influence. Only our love for our brothers and sisters can alter this equation.

Love, however, is an action verb. We cannot just hope that all will be well. It requires that we do something. And when I love someone, I will not stand idly by and watch while they destroy themselves. Nor will I remain silent in the presence of pure evil. The evil people who compose the Democrat Party leadership demand that we ignore the commandments of Jesus Christ, including love, humbleness, forgiveness, repentance, and forbearance. They prefer we live by Democrat Party edicts of constantly comparing ourselves to each other, thus justifying pride, the most damnable sin, and fomenting the destructive emotions of envy, hatred, victimization, and faithlessness in their cohorts.

In Matthew 6:24, Jesus says, "No man can serve two masters: for either he will hate one and love the other." Christians say we should "love one another." Democrats say we should "coerce one another, threaten one another, take from one another, and murder our children." Christians and Democrats, being so far apart in values and stated outcomes, cannot be currently serving the same master. Therefore, I submit to you that any Christian who has chosen to join the evil Democrat Party and follow its tenets has chosen it as their master and has knowingly or unknowingly rejected Jesus Christ.

As a Christian, I am obligated to tell you the truth. I have no control over how others feel. I can only control my perception and my behavior. As a Christian, I will not spend one moment of my time concerning myself with matters where I am powerless: racism, the weather, death, or whether others care for me. I can only control how I respond to them.

My father, Ivory Ellison, wrote a song that he and my mother, Ella Ellison, sang beautifully together as a duet: "I Wonder Is the LORD Satisfied with ME?" Too many of us are no longer concerned with that question. We should be concerned with nothing else. We should not be concerned with the views of men, Democrats, Republicans, or preachers. We should be concerned only with the opinion of GOD. Period!

There was once a time when the church said, "GOD has spoken, and the Church said: 'Amen.'" Today the church says, "GOD has spoken, and the Church says: 'Why?'" When your politics do not match your religion, you do not have a religion; you have a hobby. The present condition of the Black people, who have held fast to the coattails of the Democrat Party longer and tighter than any other people in America, bear witness to the fact that this party and the people who serve it has a master other than GOD. Are you one of them?

Because Black America does not feel loved enough by White America too many of them have been led to a state of dysfunction, self-destruction, and insanity that has made them the pity of the world. Since the implementation of the Emancipation Proclamation on January 1, 1863, Democrats have convinced most of Black America that they can only be free with the White man's permission. I refuse to travel that road. My freedom was given to me by GOD. No man and no paper have the power to give it or take it away.

Furthermore, it is an assault on my manhood to behave as most Black Democrats behave. They've become stalkers and crybabies seeking control through government coercion, a thing they cannot control, nor should they wish to prevent. These efforts toward forced compliance and acceptance should be applied more to managing oneself than managing others. As evidenced by our present environment, the former action has consistently failed and has caused its practitioners to set fire to their mothers' and grandmothers' homes. Hatred will always fail.

We must change the hearts of people. Humanity cannot achieve this change through legislation or coercion. It can be done, however, by accepting the teachings of Jesus Christ.

I cannot stomach the stalkers, cowards, and arsonists in the Democrat Party leadership for very long. Nevertheless, I will love them. I have no choice. Jesus did not give a suggestion; he gave a command.

So, how do we conquer the evil of the Democrat Party? With the love of Jesus Christ. However, unlike Adam and Eve, we will not walk blindly into the traps of Satan. This book will help you recognize and avoid the Democrats' countless snares and millions of lies. Then, with this knowledge as a weapon, attack with boldness. To quote Georges Jacques Danton: "*de l'audace, encore de l'audace, et toujours de l'audace*" (audacity, more audacity, and ever more audacity!)

It would not be wise to mistake my love for license. We each reserve the right to protect and maintain our family, our persons, and property peacefully, if possible, but with violence if necessary. The story of Christ forcibly removing thieves from his home with a whip made of cords is recorded in John 2:13 and Matthew 21:12. Possessing the power of Jesus Christ, I fear no man. If you seek to harm me or mine, to emulate Jesus's actions in the Temple: I will strike you down with righteous might and whip your ass in the name of GOD! Amen.

25 LIES

In this book, I will prove five things:

1. The Democrat Party is currently the oldest, cruelest, and most perpetually evil organization in the world. The Nazis and other racist organizations learned racism, murder, and extra-constitutionality from the Democrat Party.

2. The Democrat Party is proficient in its evil because they have willfully immersed themselves in the sin of pride and because of their unmatched ability to lie. This book will discuss twenty-five of its most damnable lies and how they have influenced hatred, racism, and death throughout the world.

3. The Democrat Party leadership does not lie to everyone. They do not need to lie to those who support their party, with full knowledge of their evil intent. These people are currently evildoers and willful agents of evil. They are beasts that walk the earth in human form.

4. Democrats must lie because most of their supporters have goodwill and are unaware of their leadership's evil intent, and when made aware of it by this book, they will leave. However, the truth will have the opposite effect on the beasts and true sadists in their party. The reality of this party's evil will increase their loyalty. To these sadists, it will be proven that you will pay a price. Make your peace with that.

5. With every past iteration of their evil, the Democrats have been defeated and will be defeated again. After we beat them this time, they will reinvent themselves as they always have, and we will defeat them again. Good will always defeat evil. It may take time. Nevertheless, it is written in John 4:7, "Submit yourselves therefore to GOD. Resist the Devil, and he will flee from you."

CHAPTER 1:

NAZIS AND DEMOCRATS—HOW I DISCOVERED THAT DEMOCRAT LEADERSHIP WAS EVIL

"The past is never dead. It's not even past."

—William Faulkner

THE GREAT AMERICAN WRITER Thomas Wolfe said, "I have to see a thing a thousand times before I see it once." I was reminded of this quote one random night in 2020 while watching a World War II documentary about Nazis. I have watched thousands of documentaries and movies documenting the evil, brutality, and inhumanity of the Nazi Party. I've read magazine articles and books, and had numerous conversations about the same. But on one random night in 2020, while up late watching one of these documentaries on the American Heroes Channel, I noticed something I had seen a thousand times but had never noticed before. *I noticed that many of the immoral tactics, motives, laws, and actions taken by the Nazis against the Jews were identical to the Jim Crow laws perpetuated against Black Americans by the Democrat Party.*

It was this night when I understood that the Democrat Party birthed the Nazi Party. I learned the German Nazi Party and the American Democrat Party were synonymous. I then understood. The DEMOCRAT PARTY IS EVIL!

After this bolt-of-lightning epiphany, I understood: The Democrat Party is not misguided. It isn't an American alternative. The Democrat Party leadership is evil and has been one of the most perpetually evil institutions in the history of the world!

It is universally agreed that the National Socialist German Workers' Party (the Nazi Party) is also one of the vilest and evilest political organizations in history. How can the Nazi Party be evil and Democrat Party not be? In two separate discussions—the first, a piece from History.com referencing Yale University's James Q. Whitman, and the second, a seminar at the United States Holocaust Memorial Museum co-led by USC Shoah Foundation's Wolf Gruner—the racism of the Democrat Jim Crow South (mistakenly called American racism) and Nazi Germany were compared and analyzed. In an effort to help you understand how egregious this whitewashing of history has been, in each statement where the author mistakenly cites America as the racist party, in parenthesis besides United States, I will insert Democrat Party. Hopefully, this will help correct the flow of disinformation. The Democrat Party in parenthesis is not part of the original text.

The History.com article explained it as, "In particular, Nazis admired the Jim Crow-era (Democrat Party) laws that discriminated against Black Americans and segregated them from white Americans, and they debated whether to introduce similar segregation in Germany." Whitman adds:

> America (the Democrat Party in America) in the early 20th century was the leading racist jurisdiction in the world. Nazi lawyers as a result, were interested in, looked very closely at, [and] were ultimately influenced by American (Democrat Party) race law.... (Democrat Party) racial classification law was much harsher than anything the Nazis themselves were willing to introduce in Germany.

In his movie *Death of a Nation*, Dinesh D'Souza makes this same observation. He said, "The Nazi Nuremberg Laws were directly modeled on the segregation laws of the Democrat Party. Every segregation law was passed by a Democrat legislature, signed by a Democratic governor, and enforced by Democrat officials. As for the Democrat one-drop rule, the Nazis found it too racist, even for them."

Becky Little, on March 20, 2019, in a piece for History.com, wrote:

> When the Nazis set out to legally disenfranchise and discriminate against Jewish citizens, they weren't just coming up with ideas out of thin air.... In particular, Nazis admired the Jim Crow-era (Democrat Party) laws that discriminated against Black Americans and segregated them from white Americans.

In *The Nazi Connection*, author Stefan Kuhl describes the impact the American eugenics movement had on Nazi thinking. In *Hitler's Ostkrieg and the Indian Wars*, author Edward B. Westermann explores the similarities between the federal Indian Removal Act (initiated almost exclusively by President Andrew Jackson and the Democrat Party) and Hitler's idea of *Lebensraum ("living space"):*

> Jim Crow laws in the American South served as a precedent in a stricter legal sense. Scholars have long been aware that Hitler's regime expressed admiration for American (Democrat Party) race law.

Pulitzer Prize–winning journalist Isabel Wilkerson in an interview with Democracy Now looks at the ways Nazi Germany borrowed from US (Democrat Party) Jim Crow laws:

> The Nazis needed no one to teach them how to hate," Wilkerson says. "But what they did was they sent researchers to the United States to study Jim Crow Laws here in the United States, to study and to research how the United States (Democrats) had managed to subordinate and subjugate its African American population.

Accordingly, it has been documented by preeminent scholars that the Democrat Party is more racist than the Nazi Party. Furthermore, that has not changed; they are still evil.

Notice how these scholars are compelled to call these racist laws "American" laws, never mentioning the Democrat Party by name. Why? Democrats are particularly good at deflecting their sins and cleansing themselves while indicting the rest of America for their crimes. With their collaborators in the liberal media, the Democrats have effectively rewritten their history. Concerning the rewriting of history regarding Nazi and Democrat Party collaboration, investigative journalist Edwin Black said to Dinesh D'Souza, in D'Souza's documentary *Death of a Nation*, "What's going on is the reshaping and falsifying of history. The Nazis also invented history. There's a role for people like me and you. We spend our lives trying to authenticate real history." And many of the good people affiliated with this evil Party are seduced by these lies. For example:

Democrat Party slaveholders are referred to only as the "slaveholders." Democrat Party traitors were called "the Confederacy." Democrat Party terrorists and liberal revolutionaries are called the "Ku Klux Klan" or "Black Lives Matter." Democrat Party liberal insurrectionists and anarchists are called "Jim Crow" or "segregationists."

Democrat Party reeducation camps are called "public schools," "colleges," and "universities." Democrat Party concentration camps and plantations are called "majority Black districts" and the "inner city." Democrat Party media is called "CNN" and "MSNBC." The Democrat Party justice department is called the "ACLU." The Democrat Party religion is called "racism," evolution," and "climate change." And Democrat Party death camps are called the "housing projects" and "Planned Parenthood."

These Jim Crow laws and Black Codes were not American codes. They were Democrat Party codes. America forced their repeal. Slavery was not an American institution. It was a Democrat Party institution. America ended slavery. The Democrat Party exclusively wielded these racists concepts, perverted Christianity, and instituted sadistic laws for their particular aims.

Nevertheless, I have been commanded to love these Democrats. Because I love them, I must warn them. Thomas Aquinas said, "We must love them both, those whose opinions we share and those whose opinions we reject." Proverbs 27:17 says, "Iron sharpens iron as a friend sharpens a friend." Luke 17:3 says, "If your brother sins rebuke him."

This book should be considered a memorandum of purpose, favoring the beginning of a new abolitionist movement paralleling the pre–Civil War abolitionist movement. Like the previous movement, this movement is designed to free the slaves and free their masters, saving them from the wrath of GOD. This new abolitionist movement will be designed to abolish the continuous slavery inflicted upon Black Americans by the Democrat Party and abolish the wall of lies that protect the Democrat leadership from the discerning sight belonging to people of goodwill.

Like our abolitionist forefathers, we will face a well-financed, highly motivated, and extremely evil Democrat Party. And in the very manner history now vindicates the actions of our abolitionist forefathers and condemns the evil of the Democrat slave masters, we will be absolved and praised for our stand, while the perennially evil Democrats will again harbor well-earned, eternal condemnation for their unyielding immorality.

Why another abolitionist movement? Aren't Black Democrats consistently crying, "WE ARE NOT FREE?" Aren't Black Democrats always claiming to be oppressed? Aren't Black Democrats claiming they are being hunted? I take them at their word. And isn't it only Democrats that still have absolute control in the Black community? Therefore, if all of these atrocities are true, Democrats must be the culprits.

The first abolitionist movement freed Black Americans only in law. But this second movement must free their minds. The first abolitionist movement required Christians to end the forced labor, murder, and oppression of their Black brethren only in law. This second abolitionist movement will convince them to end it in love. This new war for actual freedom will not be fought with guns, bombs, and bullets. This war will be fought with information. Nevertheless, it must be fought!

What is the biblical definition of evil? Proverbs 6:16–19 says, "There are six things that the LORD hates, seven that are an abomination to him." Listed below are the seven deadly sins and how the Democrat Party manifests this to everyone in deliberate practice.

1. A proud look (LGBTQ pride, Black pride, abortion pride, feminist pride)

2. "A lying tongue" (atheism, the Russia hoax, Obamacare, same-sex marriage, evolution)

3. "Hands that shed innocent blood" (sixty million abortions since 1972, disarming free citizens, ending bail, lawless inner cities)

4. "A heart that devises wicked plans" (the Big Steal 2020, impeachment, drug legalization, religious repression, euthanasia, sex change operations for children, socialism)

5. "Feet that run swiftly to evil" (rioting, burning, looting, assault, battery)

6. "A false witness that breathes out lies" (Critical Race Theory, the Russian dossier, Systemic Racism, White Privilege)

7. "One that sows discord among his brothers" (social justice, income inequality, reparations, Systemic Racism)

Can you imagine a better definition of the Democrat Party? How did the Democrats get away with this for so long? The great George Orwell wrote:

> Nazi theory indeed specifically denies that such a thing as "the truth" exists.... The implied objective of this line of thought is a nightmare world in which the Leader, or some ruling clique, controls not only the future but *the past*. If the Leader says of such and such an event, "It never happened"—well it never happened. If he says that two and two are five—well two and two are five. This prospect frightens me much more than bombs.

Democrat and Nazis say "2+2=5," and weak people follow. Only, the Nazi Party started murdering people in 1920 and was stopped in 1945. The Democrats started murdering Black people in 1800 and not only never stopped but also expanded to murdering the unborn, not just here in America but all over the world.

With the stealing of the 2020 election and the repression that followed, Democrats are pressing ever forward in expanding their "Fourth Reich" in the United States of America.

The Democrats taught the Nazis well. The Nuremberg Laws, stripping German Jews of their citizenship rights, were almost identical to the Jim Crow laws, Black Codes, laws restricting religious liberties, and proabortion laws of the Democrat Party that strip unwanted Americans of their lives. Until 1967, every anti-miscegenation law in America was enforced by a state controlled by Democrats. It took the Supreme Court decision *Loving v. Virginia* to stop it.

You say, "Well, aren't there Black leaders and Black voters in the Democrat Party?" Yes. The Black leaders in the Democrat Party are collaborators, and the voters are inmates. Isolated and abused, they have been taught to hate their liberators and their country but love their abusers. If the Jews had remained in Germany after the Holocaust, the Nazis would have convinced them that the Allied forces and the Americans were their real enemy, and Hitler was actually their friend. But the Jews had enough sense to separate themselves from their oppressors. Freed Blacks decided to stay among their racist Democrat master, and within ten years, the masters had convinced them that their liberators were their enemy.

Most Blacks are now prisoners in a one-party system. Blacks trapped in majority Black districts are no more members of the Democrat Party than Jews trapped in the German ghettos were members of the Nazi Party.

Ironically, like members of the Democrat Black Caucus, there were also Jewish collaborators in the Nazi Party. Black Americans have collaborators such as Rep. Jim Clyburn, Rep. Maxine Waters, and Sen. Raphael Warnock. The Jews had Gunther Burstyn, Adam Czerniaków, Abraham Gancwajch, Karol Hochberg, Chaim Rumkowski, Gertrude Stein, and many more.

The Nazi terrorists, the Brown Shirts, mirror the Democrat Party's terrorist wing's tactics with their Ku Klux Klan, the Red Shirts, Black Lives Matter, Antifa, and Planned Parenthood. The forced segregation, isolation, control, and exploitation of Jewish ghettos reflect the absolute hopelessness and despair of the Democrat-controlled inner cities and Southern Democrat plantations. And the infamy, terror, and wanton destruction of *Kristallnacht* reflect the carnage of the 1921 Black Wall Street riots in Tulsa, Red Summer of 1919, and the Black Lives Matter riots of 2020.

I googled "Nazis and Jim Crow." The internet lit up with information verifying my suspicions. "I had seen this thing a thousand times before I saw it once." But I had finally seen it, and now there was no doubt. The Democrat Party was the role model for the Nazi Party. Democrats taught Adolf Hitler how to implement his racism. Moreover, the Democrats had been practicing their brand of racism for almost 120 years before the Nazis ever existed and have never stopped.

The Nazis' death camps are now monuments to their cruelty. Conversely, the Democrats expanded their abortion death camps. While the Nazis' ghettos were torn down, Democrats created and maintained Black internment camps, even calling them ghettos. The Nazis' reeducation camps have been torn down. At the same time, Democrats expanded theirs and called them public schools. The Nazis can no longer repress free speech. In contrast, the Democrats are expanding the repression of speech on Google, Twitter, Facebook, and Apple. The Nazis can no longer repress religious liberty while the Democrats are expanding it by forbidding prayer in schools, shutting down church services, and imposing LGBTQ activities on citizens of faith with devout religious convictions. The Nazis can no longer confiscate weapons. At the same time, the Democrats swear to take them all.

It is an absolute, unadulterated fact that there has never been a time in history that the Nazi and Democrat Parties have not been compelled to locate the innocent and the vulnerable among them and attempt to murder them all.

THE MAKING OF A DYSTOPIA

The evil Democrat Party today reflects the same Democrat Party Abraham Lincoln described on July 4, 1861, before Congress. Like today, they were attempting to destroy this nation. Lincoln said:

> This is essentially a people's contest—On the side of the Union, it is a struggle for maintaining in the world, that form, and substance of government, whose leading object is to elevate the condition of men—to lift artificial weights from all shoulders—to clear the paths of laudable pursuit for all—to afford an unfettered start, and fair chance, in the race of life.

To the Democrat Party, that statement and that nation are blasphemous.

I understand. Some of you may say, "I vote for the Democrats because the Democrats do some good. They protect the poor, and they have more minorities in their coalition." I will respond to you by saying, "The Nazi/mass murderer, Adolf Hitler built the autobahn. The communist/atheist/mass murderer Joseph Stalin helped America defeat Hitler. Are they absolved from all their crimes?" Every evil organization has produced something that can be looked upon as a good deed. All goods deeds are washed away when one has garnered and then maintained one's power through murder, theocide, theft, and lies, as Democrats have done for over 220 years.

I know. Some of you are screaming, "Well, aren't the Republicans also evil? Don't they lie?" First of all, I am not a Republican. I do not speak for their party. I am an independent Christian Conservative, and I speak for myself. I am sure individual Republicans do lie. Nevertheless, I have yet to find anything in the Republican Party platform advocating for the murder of children, the suppression of religious expression, the violation of parental authority, the legalization of drugs, the trapping of poor children in dangerous and dysfunctional reeducation camps (public schools), the disarming of free people, the destruction of the family, or the confiscation of private property.

Even more amazing, Democrats are proud of their accomplishments and wish to expand this wasteland throughout America. I have yet to see a Republican-controlled area nearly as dysfunctional as the numerous ghettos and slums that litter America's landscape in every Democrat-controlled district with a large minority population. Yet, every election cycle, Democrats stand for reelection, celebrating this dystopia.

But I am happy to report that as long as most people in America continue to believe in GOD, this enslavement cannot be attained. Therefore, in their quest for absolute power, the Democrat Party must turn most Americans from GOD, and they have worked toward this goal for decades. In 2 Thessalonians 2:4, it is written, "The son of perdition who opposes and exalts above all that is called GOD or that is worshiped so that he sits as GOD, in the temple of GOD showing himself that he is GOD."

To all of you who are aware of the Democrat Party leadership's crimes yet continue to support this death cult, consider this book an INTERVENTION. To those who are blind, consider this book an awakening. To those whose eyes have been opened, consider this book a weapon. Make no mistake; punishment will be exacted upon the people who knowingly assist this death cult in the furtherance of its evil. These pronouncements I will prove in this book—it is necessary that I prove them. For we all agree, it is wrong and unjust that any person should be punished for ignorance. Furthermore, I earnestly hope and honestly believe that most of this party's staunchest advocates are not conscious that they are in league with pure evil. Nevertheless, a special warning must be directed to those who promote this party and benefit from its crimes while taking solace in the false belief that they have no responsibility because they did not physically light the match or pull the trigger.

The relationship between the Democrat Party and their supporters is almost identical to an organized crime or murder-for-hire syndicate, where the voter is the financier and the Democrat Party leadership is the hitman. But the financier mistakenly believes he bears zero responsibility for the hit. After reading this, you must realize that all excuses have evaporated. You are responsible. To save yourself, you must exit this evil cabal. If you do not, you will find yourself forfeit of all mercy and your eternal soul at hazard.

When the truth of the Democrat Party's centuries of evil are revealed here, anyone still furnishing aid to this party, in any way, must be viewed as a willing accomplice to murder, theft, immorality, and wanton destruction, facing an eternity in Hell as penance. These charges and punishments will not be inflicted for committing the actual crimes, but for providing aid and assistance to a known criminal, with full knowledge that this criminal was beset on limitless death and destruction.

To you who say, "I don't care about any of that because the Democrats give me free stuff." To all of you who consider yourselves Christians or at least people of goodwill, consider this: Rabbi Abraham Heschel said, "Indifference to evil is worse than evil itself." Thus, when you provide arms to the Democrat Party through your vote, empowering them to commit murder, you've become worse than a murderer because it doesn't affect you.

When a person, with knowledge or forethought, lends their hand to an organization beset on all manner of evil, they are worse than the corruption caused by this organization.

Holocaust survivor and Nobel laureate Elie Wiesel said, "The opposite of love is not hate, it is indifference.... Take sides." By not taking a side, you have taken a side: You've sided with evil. Remember, you are what you do. You will reap what you sow.

No matter your faith, it is metaphysically understood that one day you will stand before GOD. Think about what it will be like when you find yourself in his presence. Remember, if you do not leave this party and repent, you will have to be accountable to him for your complicity in the Democrat Party's theft, blasphemy, theophobia, and destruction.

Why does the Democrat Party lie? Because if Christian Conservatives reveal Democrats' true intentions, America will ostracize them. How many people would leave this party if Democrats announced that their support for abortion is not based on a woman's right to choose but is established upon the sinister foundations of eugenics, bloodlust, racism, and profit from the sale of a baby's body parts? How many people would leave the Democrat Party if the party admitted that their support for LGBTQ had nothing to do with the Fourteenth Amendment rights of citizens but was another step in a decades-long Democrat plan to destroy the family, the church, religion, and GOD? How many people would leave the Democrat Party if Conservatives revealed that Democrat support for the welfare state had nothing to do with providing economic support for Black Americans and the poor but was a mechanism utilized to control and exploit them?

I have discussed evil. But what is LOVE? Love is not just a feeling. Love is not sex. The Democrats have tried their best to turn love into something pornographic and X-rated. It is part of their schtick to turn something beautiful into something crude, vile, and ugly. They've accomplished it with family, religion, education, and community; why not love?

Love is an action verb. 1 Corinthians 13:4–5 says, "*Love is patient, love is kind. It does not envy; it does not dishonor others; it is not self-seeking; it is not easily angered; it keeps no record of wrongs.*" Romans 13:8 says, "*Owe no one anything, except to love each other, for the one who loves another has fulfilled the law.*" 1 John 4:8: "*Whoever does not love does not know GOD because GOD is love.*" John 3:16: "*GOD so loved the world that he gave his only begotten Son that who so ever believe upon him will not perish but have everlasting life.*" How do I show my love for you? By doing something.

The actions of the Democrats are described by Jesus in John 8:44 when he said: "*Ye are of your father the Devil, and the lusts of your father ye will do. He was a murderer from the beginning and abode not in the truth because there is no truth in him. When he speaketh a lie, he speaketh of his own: for he is a liar and the father of it.*"

In 1965, Paul Harvey decided to warn America because he foresaw this time in America's future when it was going to be constantly attacked, not by a foreign foe but domestically by the forces that ended up being the Democrat Party. In an attempt to knock some sense into America, he broadcasted his monumental essay "If I Were the Devil" on radios all over the country. I do not know whether or not Paul Harvey knew that by describing the identity markers of the Devil in 1965, he was describing the attributes of today's Democrat Party. The similarities are shocking. See for yourself.

Printed in the *Alabama Gazette* July 1, 2019. "If I Were the Devil" by Paul Harvey.

> If I were the devil…If I were the Prince of Darkness, I'd want to engulf the whole world in darkness. And I'd have a third of its real estate, and four-fifths of its population, but I wouldn't be happy until I had seized the ripest apple on the tree—Thee. So, I'd set about how-

ever necessary to take over the United States. I'd subvert the churches first—I'd begin with a campaign of whispers. With the wisdom of a serpent, I would whisper to you as I whispered to Eve: "Do as you please."

To the young, I would whisper that "The Bible is a myth." I would convince them that man created God instead of the other way around. I would confide that what's bad is good, and what's good is "square." And the old, I would teach to pray after me, "Our Father, which art in Washington…"

And then I'd get organized. I'd educate authors in how to make lurid literature exciting, so that anything else would appear dull and uninteresting. I'd threaten TV with dirtier movies and vice versa. I'd pedal narcotics to whom I could. I'd sell alcohol to ladies and gentlemen of distinction. I'd tranquilize the rest with pills.

If I were the devil I'd soon have families at war with themselves, churches at war with themselves, and nations at war with themselves; until each in its turn was consumed. And with promises of higher ratings I'd have mesmerizing media fanning flames. If I were the devil, I would encourage schools to refine young intellects, but neglect to discipline emotions—just let those run wild, until before you knew it, you'd have to have drug sniffing dogs and metal detectors at every schoolhouse door.

> Within a decade I'd have prisons overflowing, I'd have judges promoting pornography—soon I could evict God from the courthouse, then from the schoolhouse, and then from the houses of Congress. And in His own churches I would substitute psychology for religion, and deify science. I would lure priests and pastors into misusing boys and girls, and church money. If I were the devil I'd make the symbols of Easter an egg and the symbol of Christmas a bottle.
>
> If I were the devil I'd take from those who have, and give to those who want until I had killed the incentive of the ambitious.
>
> And what do you bet I could get whole states to promote gambling as the way to get rich? I would caution against extremes and hard work in Patriotism, in moral conduct. I would convince the young that marriage is old-fashioned, that swinging is more fun, that what you see on the TV is the way to be. And thus, I could undress you in public, and I could lure you into bed with diseases for which there is no cure. In other words, if I were the devil I'd just keep right on doing what he's doing.

I will show you their lies!

CHAPTER 2:

LIE #1—IT'S ONLY POLITICS; GOD WON'T HOLD YOU RESPONSIBLE

THERE IS A COMMON MISCONCEPTION among you who vote for and support the immoral policies of the Democrat Party. You falsely believe that there is some degree of separation regarding their actions and yours. You think that somehow because these atrocities are committed by your chosen political party and not by you specifically that you are somehow absolved and exempt from the responsibility, along with the penalties that accompany that responsibility, solely because it is political in nature.

In this chapter, we will explore the flawed logic behind this theory. I will prove:

1. Unrepented Christians and atheists will be held responsible for everything they do and say (including their votes).

2. Man's law is secondary. There is a Higher Law to which all people must answer, as well as unalienable rights untouchable by the government.

3. Evil Democrat leaders know you will not be absolved for these crimes and must lie to elicit your support.

4. Democrats want you to suffer. Their power increases with your suffering.

"But Peter and the other apostles answered and said:

'We must obey GOD rather than men.'"

—Acts 5:29

The legend of Emmett Till is an American tragedy. The truth of Emmett Till is even more of a tragedy. We know that fourteen-year-old Emmett Till was murdered on August 28, 1955, by two White men, Roy Bryant and J. W. Milam, in Money, Mississippi, for supposedly whistling at a White woman named Carolyn Bryant. Till was beaten, shot, and thrown into the river after having a cotton gin fan tied around his neck. After being found, Till's body was so disfigured that the undertaker advised a closed-coffin funeral. Till's mother, wanting to show the true face of racism, put his disfigured body on display for the world to see. The picture of his tortured body was displayed throughout the world as a sign of America's racism, and Emmet Till became a legend.

Bryant and Milam were found not guilty by an all-White male jury after only an hour of deliberation. In an act of absolute wretched pride, they sold their confession of the murder for between $3,600 and $4,000 to *Look* magazine in 1956. The part that these two White men played in the torture and murder of Emmett Till is well known, documented, and will live forever as a testament to the inhumanity of the Democrat-controlled South. Ironically, the fact that two Black men, Henry Lee Loggins and

Levi "Too Tight" Collins, also participated in Emmitt Till's murder is less known.

A lie is connected to this part of the story and viewed as fact. Black and White America seem to agree that the White men who participated in the murder of Emmitt Till should have gone to prison and should burn in Hell. Amazingly, these same people have said and believe that the adult Black male participants should be absolved by all humanity of all responsibility in this murder. Why? Because they were ordered to do it by White men. These same people who condemn Bryant and Milam absolve both Loggins and Collins as well as Mose Wright, Emmett Till's great-uncle of his paternal responsibility for allowing these White men to take his great-nephew from his home in the middle of the night without firing a shot.

Even today, you will find Black and White Americans claiming Black male cowardice as a virtue. They attempt to explain away the rape of Black women, the murder of Black children, and the buying and selling of family members in the face of their Black male protectors as something to be pitied, not despised. The fear of the Black man toward his White counterparts must be cultivated and fertilized. Indeed, on March 22, 2021, CNN debuted a documentary titled *Afraid: Fear in America's Communities of Color*. I guess I'm not part of these "Communities of Color" because I am a child of GOD and a heir of Jesus Christ. I'm not afraid of a damn thing.

During that period in our history, the viciousness and cruelty of some White men are equaled only by the cowardice and fear exhibited by most Black men. Yet history condemns the White man's ruthlessness while concurrently justifying and rationalizing the Black man's fear and submission. *In this historical and now present telling of this story lie a tacit admission, approval, and expectation that Black men are inferior to White men and will always be dominated, beaten, and murdered by them.* Even now, when it comes to income, crime, SAT scores, incarceration rates, and so forth. Black Americans are convinced that they should constantly compare themselves to White Americans. Sadly, most Black Americans view this inferiority as a virtue—a badge of redemptive suffering. The Democrat Party has always rewarded this type of slave-minded behavior and actively recruited Black men willing to reinforce it to the Black masses. Indeed, the March 30, 2021, edition of the *Washington Post*'s front page paraded a color picture of prominent Black men on their knees at the Derek Chauvin trial.

These Black Democrat leaders have concluded that the Democrat Party, continuing as the Black man's benevolent master and masquerading as his Superman protector, is his only hope. It is time for the Black community to understand *SUPERMAN IS NOT COMING. BUT JESUS IS HERE!*

Consequently, Black men like me who cannot acknowledge any man as my superior and only GOD as my master are viewed by Democrats as a problem. We are flies in the ointment. It is necessary that most Black people and most of America must agree with this absolute submissive premise of Democrat Party governance and ideology: cowardice and submission in the body of the White man will be looked upon with absolute disgust but viewed as virtuous in the body of Black Americans.

The mental and physical castration of Black men has always been one of the Democrat's ultimate goals. However, a higher law has demanded that men keep their manhood. Most Black men have failed at this. Like all men who allow beasts to eat the flesh of their children: they will be held accountable.

As Americans tell our history to the world, the heroic deeds of the White men we celebrate are connected to their gallantry in war and conflict. Conversely, the heroism of Black people is celebrated in those who coveted the company, affirmation, and social equality with their so-called White oppressors. Even today,

Democrats are still surprised to celebrate the first Black person to achieve a White man's standard, like with Gen. Lloyd J. Austin III, Joe Biden's nominee for secretary of defense, who happens to be Black and highly qualified. We celebrate as heroes those who suffered and died to sit in the company of White people and beg for the approval of racists. In these celebrations exist the tacit acknowledgment of Black inferiority. Worst of all, it imparts permission upon weak Black men to remain weak and never fulfill their destiny as true mighty men of GOD.

The beliefs of White Americans or any person are of no consequence. But, for any Christian of any race to believe in their own inferiority in the presence of other men is an affront to GOD.

Imagine the expression on the faces of the Black men who killed Emmett Till when they discovered that the orders of the real GOD supersede the demands of their White GOD. The orders of their White GOD will not absolve them. I trust many Christian Democrats will have the same expression when they make the same discovery. We will all be held accountable.

This accountability exists because GOD'S law is paramount. This theory was to be played out in the pre–Civil War United States Senate.

A HIGHER LAW

On March 11, 1850, Southern Democrats in the United States of America mainly allowed White people to use their state governments' authority to keep Black people in a subordinate and depraved condition of indentured servitude. Most people (called slaves) resided in the southern part of the United States and were owned almost exclusively by Democrats. The northern part of the country was mainly free to all citizens, Black and White. Even though this sick arrangement had been the case since the nation's independence on July 4, 1776, on March 11, 1850, one US senator had had enough and was going to let his feelings be known to the nation and the world.

His name was William Seward, a Republican from the state of New York. He was going to give a speech defining his opposition, not only to the extension of slavery but to slavery itself. His address would change American history.

Seward acknowledged the Constitution permitted and protected slavery where it existed but argued that the territories were governed by a "higher law" than the Constitution. He explained that this was a moral law, established by "the creator of the universe." Furthermore, he demanded that California be admitted as a free state and informed the South that slavery was doomed.

The speech catapulted Seward to international fame. He was hated and ridiculed by slaveholding Democrats in the South for even assuming a "higher power" than the Constitution. Even though most Southern Democrats considered themselves Christians, they knew that the doctrine of "higher law" would cost them their earthly power.

Today's Democrats have devolved. They now consider Marxist ideology higher than the Constitution and higher law than the laws of GOD. Their support for abortion, LGBTQ, drug legalization, pornography, secular education, and general oppression verify, 170 years later, that the Democrat Party has become more immoral and even more barbaric.

Seward's speech lifted the doctrine of "higher law" into the vernacular of American politics and helped lay the foundation for the Civil War and the Thirteenth, Fourteenth, and Fifteenth Amendments that followed. Seward served as Abraham Lincoln's secretary of state and helped lead the country after Lincoln's death.

The idea of a law higher than the laws on this earth isn't a new concept. And the opposition to it by satanic Democrat leadership has never changed. The Democrats believed then and believe now that man's law should take precedence over the laws of GOD. They also demand that we submit to this blasphemy or be punished by the government. The execution of this flawed concept has led to untold misery. Slavery, Jim Crow, genocide, and the violation of every unalienable right are offsprings of this blasphemy.

Is there any circumstance where a person can knowingly facilitate innocent murder and not be held responsible? Is there any circumstance where a person can sanction the use of force or coercion in an effort to separate any human being from their GOD or from practicing their religion in the way they see fit and not be held accountable? Is there any circumstance where any human being can justifiably force another human being to disarm in a world crowded with murderers and thieves and not carry the weight of their spilled blood? Is there any circumstance where a person will not be held responsible when they knowingly protect sadistic adults who corrupt the minds of children and mutilate their bodies with drugs and castration, falsely claiming that they have changed their genders to something more accommodating to the adult's liking?

Some of you enjoy participating in evil, and you know it. You do not seek GOD or man's absolution. You cannot sleep unless you do evil or cause someone to stumble. Then there are you who mistakenly believe that politics provide a protected veneer. You actually believe that you are good people and you will only be judged by what you do in your personal lives. Wielding politics as a shield, you believe that you are one step removed from the crime. You believe this one step allows you "deniability."

I've coined the flawed logic "the Slaughterhouse Principle." The Slaughterhouse Principle is straightforward. You don't enjoy killing the cow and grinding its flesh, but you love hamburgers. Consequently, some ambitious entrepreneur who doesn't mind getting his hands bloody builds a slaughterhouse and provides you with your burger minus the nauseating carnage.

While practicing this principle, you've mentally protected yourself from the savagery of the act and thus believe that you can't have accountability.

With most Democrats, the Slaughterhouse Principle has been applied politically: You didn't actually kill the baby, leave a law-abiding citizen helpless, forbid the old lady from praying, or castrate the child. Therefore, you shouldn't be held accountable. This flawed logic is a fatal mistake. Nowhere in the laws of GOD or man does this veneer exist. You will be held responsible.

Similar to rape and murder during times of war, many soldiers have suffered execution after discovering the uniform, and the orders did not absolve them from responsibility. Many of you will have the same surprise. There is a "higher law!" Like many of those sadistic officers, Democrat leaders know you are not exempt. But they care nothing for you. All they do is meditate on blood: the more blood, the better. Your blood is added to the total.

To the serpent, Eve explained that she was not permitted to eat from the tree of knowledge; for the day that she ate from it, she would surely die. The serpent, needing Eve to disobey a direct order from GOD, provided her false immunity; he replied in Genesis 3:1, "Yeah hath God said, Ye shall eat of every tree in the garden?" he then said in Genesis 3:4, "You will not surely die." Satan taught the Democrats well. They provide false immunity and false security too. But without repentance, Eve was held responsible: because she did die.

The serpent cared nothing for Eve; you must realize the Democrat Party cares nothing for you. Satan tempted Jesus with scripture until Christ told him to "get thee behind me, Satan." Now he lies to you. He says, "It is only politics. You have a right to choose." "You have the right to marry whom you love." "You have a right not to be offended." "You have a right to mutilate your child." "You will not be held responsible." "You will not surely die."

A criminal once told me everyone he had ever partnered with in crime had larceny in his heart. They would not steal, but they would buy stolen goods from him. They wouldn't traffic or sell drugs but had no problem purchasing them from him. He never conducted criminal activity with an honest man. His customers mistakenly believed that this one degree of separation gave them severability. In the eyes of the law, they quickly discover the flaw in their hypothesis.

Likewise, many of you that vote for the Democrat Party already have larceny in your hearts. It is the Slaughterhouse Principle: You won't wring the chicken's neck, but you love your McNuggets. You will not steal from your neighbor, but you will vote for the Democrats to steal on your behalf. You will not murder a child, but you will vote for the Democrat Party to murder on your behalf. You will not disarm a neighbor, but you will vote for the Democrat Party to disarm them on your behalf. You would not prohibit your neighbor from expressing their religion freely, but you will vote for the Democrats to do it on your behalf. They lie to you, and you take comfort when they say, "You will not surely die."

Sooner or later, you will realize because of your passive-aggressive hatred that your life hasn't gotten any better. You will find yourself physically and spiritually impoverished. Many of you have been burdened with this hatred for so long you cannot imagine what it is like to be free of it. Every time you find yourself siding with the Democrats regarding these issues of life and death, it will help for you to remember what it will be like when the tally is taken, and your payment is due.

Nevertheless, I am comforted and stand firm on the words of King David when he said in Psalms: 146:3–4 (ESV), "*Put not your trust in princes, in a son of man, in whom there is no salvation.*"

All this matters little to Democrat Leaders. When GOD "appointed" kings, he held them responsible for the actions of their government. In the United States, "We the People" are the sovereign. We do not have government leaders. We have servants. You cannot be held responsible for the actions of your leader, but you are held accountable for the actions of your servant.

For this reason, politicians provide you with this false sense of security by proclaiming themselves your leaders, knowing under our republican form of government that "leaders" are an anathema. Worst of all, many of you believe it. These politicians are your "servants." When you believe these politicians are your leaders and not your servants, you then provide your servants/politicians with unlimited power, while walking away with a false sense of immunity, unaware of the fact that you are on your way to Hell.

How do Democrats justify such heresy? They claim that we allow religion to govern our private lives, and we allow politics to control our public lives. They claim this exemption based on the fact that we do have a secular government. A government guided by our Constitution, not by our Bibles.

However, the higher law doctrine and concept of unalienable rights contradict this theory entirely. The higher law doctrine explained simply says: even though we have a secular government, we acknowledge that any Biblical or religious doctrine doesn't control this secular government and that it is, in fact, controlled by its people. Ergo, the values of the people will be reflected in their government.

"The devil can cite Scripture for his purpose."

—William Shakespeare, *The Merchant of Venice*

"Who are you to judge?" "Only GOD can judge me!" "Judge not so you will not be judged." You will find these to be the most oft-repeated Bible verses for Democrats. The second is "Do unto others as you will have them do unto you." The third (even though it is not scripture): "Who are you to throw stones?"

Democrats attack anyone who dares question their immoral behavior. It matters not to them that these scriptures are taken entirely out of context. Democrats utilize them with prideful intent. They never recite these scriptures to rebuke and correct hypocrisy as intended. On the contrary, because of their pride and their intent to inflict harm, Democrats recite these holy scriptures to defend their immoral behavior against correction and deflect criticism, placing criticism upon the person who dares call them to account.

Love everyone. Be kind to everyone. And because you love them, rebuke your brothers and sisters with kindness and grace, only after first receiving their permission. But understand, you cannot help anyone who does not desire help. Help those who seek it. To all the others, turn them over to GOD.

CHAPTER 3:

LIE #2—THE DEMOCRAT PARTY WANTS TO STOP SEGREGATION

IF DEMOCRATS PREFER INTEGRATION over segregation, why are there dozens of Democrat-controlled majority-Black Congressional districts? Why are there hundreds of Democrat-controlled, majority-Black inner city ghettos? Why are there thousands of Democrat-controlled majority-Black public schools that are failing? Could it be that Democrats prefer segregation?

In this chapter, I will prove:

1. White Democrats invented legal segregation by race in America.

2. Black and White Democrats invented de jure segregation and want it expanded.

3. Segregation helps the Iron Triangle (comprising most Black preachers, Black politicians, and Black civic organizers) and the Democrat Party maintain their power.

4. Democrat Party governance is the problem in the Black community, not segregation.

5. Even though it has no intrinsic value, Democrats propose forced integration as valuable to the Black community and present themselves as the only organization able to deliver it.

"Insanity: Doing the same thing over and over again and expecting a different result."

—Unknown

In 1989, newly appointed Republican National Committee (RNC) Chairman Lee Atwater had a problem. Democrats were in charge of the House of Representatives, and he wanted to flip it to the Republicans. Atwater decided to tackle the problem of congressional redistricting. But since Democrats controlled most state legislatures and those legislatures controlled the redistricting process, he was in trouble. Atwater came up with a plan.

This plan is chronicled in the June 26, 2016, edition of the *New Yorker* magazine:

> He assigned the task to…Ben Ginsberg. The "something" Ginsberg came up with was an appeal to the Congressional Black Caucus.
>
> The caucus didn't have much reason to listen to the RNC. At the time, it had zero Republican members (and today it has just one). But Ginsberg argued that when it came to redistricting—or, from another perspective, gerry-

> mandering—the two groups shared a common interest. How about if they collaborated?
>
> The pitch worked. *The RNC and the Congressional Black Caucus joined forces to press for the creation of more majority-black districts.* [Author's italics] These districts were drawn so as to concentrate, or "pack," African American voters, a move that had a dramatic and possibly permanent effect. Consider the example of Georgia. In 1990, the state sent nine Democrats to Congress. Eight of them were white; the ninth was the civil rights leader, John Lewis. In 1994, the state sent three African-Americas to Congress. The trade-off was that only one white Democrat got elected (and he switched parties five months later). Perhaps not coincidentally, in 1994, Republicans took control of the House. In an interview with this magazine the following year, Ginsberg said he was convinced that the alliance with the Black Caucus had been crucial to the G.O.P.'s victory. Asked if the strategy had had a name, he said no, then jokingly suggested "Project Ratfuck."

Since Republican candidates in these majority-Black districts receive minimal, if any, support from the RNC, I believe it is common sense to conclude that the RNC hasn't really funded a candidate representing the Republican Party in these minority districts in thirty years. The vast majority-Black community, therefore, hasn't had any interaction with the Republican Party for the past thirty years. Consequently, the Democrats have had absolute control of these districts since "Operation Ratf*%K."

They have used this power to cement their control by injecting a foreign and unnatural culture among the people. The "hip-hop" culture of sex, violence, and materialism has taken hold. And the apostate teaching of Black Liberation Theology has left the "real" church too compromised to combat it. Democrats maintain this dystopia and their power through segregation and will never willingly give it up. The liberal press has always deflected their party's complicity in race segregation by laying it at the feet of hapless Republicans, who will happily take the blame if it ensures a continual Black absence in their majority-White districts. The press must hide the fact that the party to which most of them belong has been given absolute power to either make an oasis of these areas or turn them into deserts.

As with North and South Korea and East and West Germany, this was a contest against socialist ideas versus capitalism. And capitalism has won hands down. Democrats now must confiscate taxes from conservative areas to bail out these dysfunctional, poverty-ridden inner cities and segregated Democrat-controlled areas. The Democrat Party members are slumlords and poverty pimps who started, maintained, and greatly benefited from de jure racial segregation here in America.

Even though Black Democrats pretend to covet integration, they fight viciously in courts of law and in the back rooms of statehouses to maintain the Black exclusivity and segregation of these majority-minority districts. Republicans do the same, but Republican action is well known and usually draws disfavor. Black Democrats pretend to be the victims. As if out of the spirit of fair play, any of them would willfully give up their majority-Black districts and allow a White Democrat to take their place.

But according to liberals, Blacks must be the victims because they are not as shrewd, cruel, or cunning as their fearful White counterparts. Electing fewer America-hating Democrats to the United States government would be the only redeeming value to forced integration. Instead, the segregation and isolation of Black Americans on Democrat-controlled plantations, now called majority-Black districts and the inner city, continue to be the Democrat Party's primary tool of control.

Remember, Thomas Wolfe said, "I have to see a thing a thousand times before I see it once." I am reminded of that statement whenever I pass through a housing project nestled in the heart of the ghetto of every big city in America. For decades, I drove daily through these hellholes believing they were a visual symbol of White oppression in America. I now know they are a symbol of Democrat Party control and the Black Iron Triangle's power. The Black Democrat power structure, as described previously, benefits from this segregation.

To perpetually receive 90 percent of the Black vote, the Democrat Party leadership has invented a society where it is not only acceptable but fashionable for Black people to hate one another. Thomas Wolfe said, "Culture is the arts elevated to a set of beliefs." Regarding the Black community, it is an unadulterated fact that the art elevated by the Democrat-controlled media depicts Blacks as violent, immoral, poverty-stricken, ignorant, antisocial, and fratricidal. Now, just as Thomas Wolfe said, this art has been elevated to a set of beliefs where, whenever a large group of Black Americans live together in close proximity, they rape, assault, exploit, and kill each other on an industrial scale. Understandably, this causes other races to keep their distance. De jure segregation is the result and the intention.

This exploitation is nothing new. Whether they are Indian reservations, Jewish ghettos, or Black Democrat plantations, the process and execution are identical. First, identify the group of people you intend to oppress. Second, isolate those people. Third, control all information in and out of the area. Fourth, control the economics or "who gets what" in the area. Fifth, control the education in the area. Sixth, control the politics in the area. Seventh, now you control everything in the area. Democrats have been doing this for years and have perfected the process.

Most telling, as the violence and dysfunction in the Black community escalate, the Democrat Party continues to expand their poisonous cultural influence by increasing the Black community's exposure to sex, drugs, violence, materialism, and theocide. Ironically, while most other races attempt to treat the Black community with compassion and understanding, the hatred destroying the Black community is expressed almost exclusively from within its own family. The hatred that Black Americans inflict upon one another is a phenomenon that initiates marvel and confusion around the world. This cultural genocide has been skillfully planned and faithfully executed by the Democrat Party. Sadly, it has worked remarkably well for the past 220 years.

Using this as a backdrop, it may help you to understand why the Democrat Party leadership maintains and violently resists any change to segregation on the basis of race while simultaneously pretending that they abhor it.

Surprisingly, Black people living among other Black people is not the problem and never has been. Like East Germans living under the Communists, Black people living under the control of one the most perpetually evil institutions in the history of the world is the problem. Democrats, like communists, use segregation as a tool of power, control, exploitation, and isolation. With this isolation and control, Democrats, like the communists, can then blame the intentionally devastating outcomes of their leadership on forces locked out of the Black community who do not have a voice and cannot defend themselves. Communists blamed America. Democrats like their communist brothers also blame America, but they also blame Republicans, evangelicals, Fox News, Rush Limbaugh, and so on.

Segregation, therefore, should no longer be defined as the separation of Blacks from the rest of America. This has a negative connotation. I repeat, just as there is nothing wrong with East Germans living among East Germans, Whites living among Whites, and Asians living among Asians, there is nothing wrong with Black people living among other Black people. *It is not the color of their skin that causes their dysfunction but the evil system that is forced upon them.*

Segregation, therefore, should be redefined as such: A system where one-party rule is preserved by force after a political party intentionally and artificially separates a population from its natural streams of support. It then enslaves that population by successfully corrupting the arts, which are responsible for creating and maintaining their beliefs. The annihilation of their culture and the obliteration of their institutions are the result of this corruption. The instilling of that single political party with perpetual absolute authority becomes a reality, and the segregation and exploitation of that population become indefinite.

Segregation is not evil because of race or ideological separation. People of the same nationality, race, religion, or political ideology naturally congregate together. Segregation is evil when politicians artificially manage, encourage, and maintain this separation with disinformation, intimidation, oppression, hatred, and fear, all to gain and maintain power. It is augmented when one's inferiority is contrived to justify the separation.

To say that you "choose" to remain separate because you choose to assemble only with those you love and enjoy or because you fear and hate the outside world does at least guarantee civility and respect among the segregated groups. But to be told, as Democrats tell Black people, that you are "forced" to be separated because you are Black, despised, and unwanted will produce a self-fulfilling prophesy, where you not only learn to hate yourself but everyone that looks like you. Thus, Democrats have intentionally created these inner city, Mad Max dystopias, where the only uncommon act is the act of civility.

The arts are intended to uplift humanity, strengthen institutions, perpetuate harmony, encourage piety, favor commerce, and instill self-worth. But when political segregation is implemented, the arts are employed to destroy institutions, instill hatred, reject religious instruction, seek idleness, and relish in self-abuse. The unchanging leadership of these dystopias is clear evidence of the "learned helplessness" forced upon these abused citizens by their political representatives: communists or Democrats—one and the same.

The Democrats do not want to end the segregation of the races. They want to expand it.

CHAPTER 4:

LIE #3—THE DEMOCRAT PARTY IS BASED ON LOVE

THE LOVE OF A MASTER for his slave is the only love allowed by the Democrat Party leadership. Since its inception, the Democrat Party has been an organization whose primary objective is to seize power for its leadership by subjugating, impoverishing, enslaving, and terrorizing those under their jurisdiction and control. If the Democrat Party loves anything, history proves that it loves to destroy.

Is the Democrat Party a party of love? We will discuss that.

In this chapter, I will prove:

1. The Democrat Party policies are almost identical to the policies of the Communist Party of the United States.

2. Policies from the Democrat Party have destroyed cities and states where Democrats garner control.

3. The entire history of the Democrat Party's politics has rested on promoting hate, division, and death.

4. Their leadership consists of a cabal of psychotics.

> The Captain: "*You gonna get used to wearin' those chains after while, Luke. Don't you never stop listenin' to them clinking. 'Cause they gonna remind you of what I been saying. For your own good.*"
>
> Luke: "*Wish you'd stop being so good to me, Captain.*"

The above quote is from the movie *Cool Hand Luke*. Luke was a prisoner sentenced to a Southern prison chain gang. The captain of the prison had one goal, to break Luke for Luke's own good. But Luke understood that his being broken would only benefit the captain, thus the quote.

Blacks, Hispanics, single mothers, prison inmates, crack heads, inner city children, government school children, and illegal aliens, aren't you tired of Democrats "being so good to you"? You know I'm being facetious.

The great C. S. Lewis was quoted as saying:

> Of all tyrannies, a tyranny sincerely exercised for the good of its victim may be the most oppressive. It may be better to live under robber barons than under omnipotent moral busybodies. The robber baron's cruelty may sometimes sleep, his cupidity may at some point be satiated, but those who torment us for our own good will torment us without end, for they do so with the approval of their own conscience.

George Orwell's *Animal Farm* is an allegorical book written to reflect the events leading to the Russian Revolution. Orwell uses an animal farm as a microcosm of a totalitarian nation and uses animals as citizens of this nation. The hardworking, naïve, and ignorant horse named Boxer symbolizes the abused and uneducated masses. He is a loyal supporter of the self-appointed tyrant, a pig named Napoleon, and his fellow pigs that make up the leadership. He listens to everything Napoleon says and always responds "Napoleon is always right." When Boxer collapses from overwork, the pigs send him to the knacker's yard to be slaughtered in exchange for money to buy a case of whiskey for themselves. Napoleon and the pigs honored Boxer in front of the farm inhabitants and reminded the farm that Boxer said, "Napoleon is always right."

Sadly, Boxer reminds me of Black people in a Democrat Party controlled by pigs. The conditions in the Democrat-controlled inner cities verify that Democrats view these people as cannon fodder. Their purpose is to protest, vote, use neighborhoods for organized crime, and allow Democrats to monetize their existence for unions (public education, abortions, social services, law enforcement, health care, food stamps, housing, and so on). According to Michelle Ye Hee Lee in a December 5, 2014 article for the *Washington Post*, it costs America approximately $35,000 for Democrats to keep one person poor with welfare benefits. If college grants and all the above services are added, one can see how it could cost the Democrats close to $100,000 to keep one American poor. Consistent with their robber baron mentality, in 2021, Democrats borrowed over $14,500 per citizen to give each citizen $1,400 for the $1.9 trillion coronavirus stimulus bill. The rest was used as a payoff to friends, unions, and special interests.

Look around you. Nothing indicates that the Democrat Party has anything to do with love. We've examined what the Bible says about evil. What does it say about love? Love is described in 1 Corinthians 13:4-5:

> Love is patient; love is kind. It does not envy.
> It does not boast, it is not proud. It does not

> dishonor others, it is not self-seeking, it is not easily angered, it keeps no record of wrongs.

With that definition as evidence, and the Democrats Party's admittance to its participation in the murder of children, slogans of "No Justice, No Peace," covetousness, religious repression, calls for reparations, demands for apologies, and their rewriting of history, I believe I am justified in saying without any equivocation, that the Democrat Party is a party of absolute HATE!

The communist program for America and the Democrat program for America are identical. A few of the many points where they agree:

1. $15.00 minimum wage

2. National universal health insurance

3. Increased taxes on the rich and corporations

4. Strong regulations on the financial industries

5. Regulation and ownership of utilities

6. Increased federal aid to cities and states

7. Reduced military budget

8. Civil rights expansion

9. Campaign finance reform

10. Election law reform

11. Wealth redistribution

12. Affirmative action

13. Support for global warming initiatives

14. LGBTQ dominion

According to its Wikipedia page, the Communist Party of the United States of America's membership lies between five and ten thousand. Where are all the communists? They've fled to the Democrat Party, transforming the party of JFK and Harry S. Truman into something unrecognizable.

A list of grievances, claims of discrimination, threats of reprisals, and demands for pity are all the Democrats have to offer. Forcing America to live in a state of absolute condemnation is their solution. The fact that everywhere it has been implemented, their ideology has led to nothing but misery, poverty, and death is precisely why they seek to execute it. The Democrat Party is a death cult.

Democrat-controlled cities like Detroit, Milwaukee, Philadelphia, San Francisco, Memphis, New Orleans, and Portland are crime ridden, in debt, and dying. Nevertheless, the Democrats who control these cities pridefully stand for reelection every two years. Why? The condition of the cities is intentional. If they do enough damage, like Kamala Harris, Jim Clyburn, and Cory Booker, they get promoted.

Remember, the origins of this party began in nullification, division, and succession. It continued in racism, hate, the Confederacy, and the Civil War. It currently remains in religious repression, atheism, racism, division, hatred, and murder.

Where is the love in the Democrat Party leadership? They want to change America. Therefore, they can't love it. They want to pass laws that encourage drug use, euthanasia, gun confiscation, prostitution, Marxism, and abortion. They, therefore, do not love mankind. What do they love? They love power. They love evil.

Senator Daniel Webster was quoted as saying:

> Good intentions will always be pleaded for every assumption of authority. It is hardly too strong to say that the Constitution was made to guard the people against the dangers of good intentions. There are men in all ages who mean to govern well, but they mean to govern. They promise to be good masters, but they mean to be masters.

In the future, whenever a Democrat leader says he wants to help you, remember *Cool Hand Luke*. And just say, "I wish you'd stop helping me, Captain."

CHAPTER 5:

LIE #4—LGBTQ IS ALL ABOUT EQUALITY

LESBIAN, GAY, BISEXUAL, TRANSGENDER, and queer people are children of GOD and American citizens. As with all of us in the human family, they should be treated with love, respect, and dignity while being afforded equal protection under the law. Nevertheless, a schism and conflict exists between certain components of the LGBTQ-preferred lifestyle, the doctrines of most traditional mainstream religions, and the people who fervently practice and strive to be obedient to these religious doctrines.

This conflict increases their value exponentially to Democrat Party leaders who want to destroy and change America by persecuting those who believe in GOD, thereby depriving America of His blessings and protections. Democrat leaders cannot harm our nation, or us, until we Christians voluntarily reject GOD. The unbridgeable conflict between LGBTQ life and Christianity is the conflict Democrats have chosen that gives them the best chance at destroying Christianity in America.

In this chapter, I will prove:

1. As with Black people, the Democrat leaders care nothing about the well-being of LGBTQ persons. They are another tool in their effort to destroy America.

2. Many LGBTQ persons do not support the LGBTQ or Democrat Party agenda.

3. As with the Black community, the Democrat Party encourages the sin of pride in the LGBTQ community as fuel to foster non-repentance, thus separating America from GOD.

4. Religious freedom supersedes every other Constitutional right.

5. Democrats are exploiting the LGBTQ community in the United States in an effort to implement the "Daniel Test" separating America from GOD.

6. Democrats have always feared the Black male and have always sought to either kill or emasculate him. They are pressing the LGBTQ agenda to forward this evil plan.

"The family is threatened by growing efforts

On the part of some to redefine the very

Institution of marriage, by relativism, by the culture

Of the ephemeral, by lack of openness to life."

—Pope Francis

In his article "The Myth of the Impotent Black Male," Robert Staples writes:

> In White America there is a cultural belief that the Black community is dominated by its female members, its men having been emasculated by historical vicissitudes of slavery and contemporary economic forces. This cultural belief contains a duality of meaning; that black men have been deprived of their masculinity and that black women participated in the emasculinization process.

Democrats hate independent, fearless, responsible Christian Black men like my father and me. Impotent, obedient, emasculated, and servile Black men are more to their liking. Speaker of the House Nancy Pelosi has no trouble controlling the Black men in the Democrat Party for this reason. These men are emasculated men who are destroying their own people under orders from Mistress Nancy.

To control Black America, men like us must be minimized. Murder, prison, failed education, drug abuse, fatherlessness, and unemployment are tools previously used to bring about our demise. But the most dangerous weapon ever unleashed on Black men by the Democrat Party is the LGBTQ agenda.

The Democrats celebrating winning the culture war is equivalent to a patient celebrating a cancer diagnosis. Nevertheless, the evidence suggests that the Democrats are winning and are getting the desired effect. A story in the February 24, 2021, edition of *USA Today* reported that "a record 5.6% of US adults identify as LGBTQ, poll shows." The story is jubilant at the finding that so many young people are accepting this lifestyle. It reads:

> One of the biggest headlines in the 2020 poll is the emergence of Generation Z adults, those 18 to 23: 1 in 6 or 15.9%, identify as LGBTQ. In each older generation, LGBTQ identification is lower, including 2% or less of respondents born before 1965.... 54.6% identify as bisexual...24.5% identify as gay; 11.7% identify as lesbian; 11.3% identify as transgender.

On March 30, 2021, the 700 Club's Pat Robertson reported that Planned Parenthood had decided to start offering "Gender Affirming Therapy" targeting children sixteen and under. Heather Sells, a reporter for the 700 Club, reported:

> Planned Parenthood has begun offering hormone therapy to those who identify as transgender. It is a new business model that makes financial sense potentially for years to come.... The abortion provider's annual report shows its expanding business venture. Two hundred centers in 31 states now welcome these young people, and the Family Research Council says Planned Parenthood has become the second largest provider of hormone therapy to those wanting to change. It is labeled "Gender Affirming Therapy," which means no questions asked and no need for mental health support.... Some centers are targeting teenagers 16 and under, setting up a business relationship that can last a lifetime and permanently alter adolescent bodies.

Pat Robertson continued to opine:

> The founder of Planned Parenthood is Margaret Sanger. She was unbelievably evil. She wrote a book, and don't tell me it's not true because I read it. It's called *Breeding the Thoroughbred.* She wanted to sterilize mentally defectives, Southern European people, certain Protestants, and of course she wanted to sterilize Black people. That was her agenda. And Planned Parenthood was the founder of what is called eugenics. I thought she had taken her agenda from Adolf Hitler but it's the other way around. And Planned Parenthood has gotten so pervasive and has taken so much money from the federal government that Barak Obama, during his presidency in a showdown with Congress, was willing to shut down the federal government rather than eliminate some of the money that is being paid to Planned Parenthood.... It amounts to at least one hundred thousand dollars and maybe more. It is an evil organization.

Coincidentally, Margaret Sanger was an ardent Democrat. Hillary Clinton and Nancy Pelosi have been past recipients of the Margaret Sanger Award.

What is this obsession White male Democrats have with castrating Black men? According to a *Vice* article, the Equal Justice Initiative, "while there aren't comprehensive statistics for the number of black men castrated by white mobs, experts say that white men's fear of black male sexuality lead to a constant threat of violence, including castration, from the time of slavery to the mid-twentieth century."

In a speech, Dick Gregory reported that the great inventor from the Tuskegee Institute, Dr. George Washington Carver, as a young slave, was castrated by his Democrat master because of Washington's proximity to the master's daughters. When the FBI dug up the bodies of Michael Schwerner, Andrew Goodman, and James Chaney, they discovered that the Black man, Chaney, had been castrated by his White male Democrat Ku Klux Klan murderers. In movie the *Free State of Jones*, freed slave Moses Washington decides to register other freedmen to vote for the Republican Party. A gang of White Democrats hang him and castrate him. Not knowing that this graphic scene would be in the movie, I attempted to hide it from my then ten-year-old daughter.

Nevertheless, she understood what the White Democrats had done to Moses Washington. Knowing that my politics closely matched his, my ten-year-old daughter asked me if the Democrats would do the same thing to me. I responded, *"Not as long as I have Jesus Christ and my gun!"* Nothing has changed. Democrats still seek to castrate every Black man they can find. Except, for today, the castration is now mental but just as effective.

In "Sex, Drugs, and…Race-to-Castrate: A Black Box Warning of Chemical Castration's Potential Racial Side Effects," in the *Harvard BlackLetter Law Journal* (volume 25, 2009), Marques P. Richeson wrote, "The social oppression and castration of black men is rooted in race and gender.… Currently, a handful of states have enacted chemical castration laws applicable to offenders of sex crimes. The phenomenon of chemical castration, in turn, threatens to serve as a tool of white domination insofar as it possesses the kinetic energy to perpetuate and further entrench black male subordination." The castration occurred to bear witness to the virility of the White male and the undergirding of White power.

The castration of Black males is a vulgar and evil phenomenon previously and presently practiced by Democrat leaders. It can be conducted physically, mentally, or chemically. In the past, Democrats were honest. They called Black people nigger while they isolated Black Americans on plantations and ghettos, deprived them of their right to vote, gave them substandard education, destroyed their families, and incarcerated and castrated their men.

The Democrats haven't changed a thing. But they are allowed to get away with it because they've changed their rhetoric, not their actions. Like a verbally and physically abusive husband now saying he loves his wife while he beats her, Democrats have found that they can get away with any form of racism as long as they say, "We are doing it for the Black community's benefit," and as long as they no longer publicly say nigger.

Because White Democrats no longer call them nigger they have been allowed to expand their destruction unmolested, adding AIDS, religious repression, abortion, and LGBTQ to the equation.

At the end of the day, Black men are doing this to themselves. They delivered their children to their Democrat enemies to educate and then feigned surprise when the White racist Democrats taught them to hate themselves. On August 29, 2019, Nature.com reported in an article called, "No 'gay gene': Massive study homes in on genetic basis of human sexuality":

> Nearly half a million genomes reveal five DNA markers associated with sexual behavior—but none with the power to predict the sexuality of an individual.

Because we love our LGBTQ brothers and sisters, we must tell them the truth. Even though we love them, we must remind ourselves that there isn't any known evidence that any LGBTQ behaviors are genetic. As a matter of fact, in his book *The Homosexual Matrix*, C. A. Tripp argues that sexual orientation is not innate and depends on learning. He said people do not become homosexual based on things like hormone levels, fear of the opposite sex, or the relationship with the parent. He surmised that controlling erotic feelings depends on the willingness to resist. This attitude was reinforced on March 16, 2021, when the *Washington Post* reported on the very liberal Pope Francis and the Catholic Church's 2,000-year teachings on homosexuality. It reported that the pope said same-sex unions can't be blessed. The pronouncement also stated that same-sex unions are not ordered to the Creator's plan and those unions are illicit. It says that GOD "cannot bless sin."

If you are a Catholic, this pronouncement from what some have called a very liberal and nontraditional pope should settle the question. If you consider yourself a Christian, this pronouncement should carry tremendous weight. But it is hard to resist when members of the Democrat Party who are Protestant and Catholic and who wield power in the church, politics, and schools continually tell you that you now live in a consequence-free society. It encourages the very young to do whatever makes them feel good.

Consequently, the American birthrate has been declining since 2009, when the Democrat Party decided to indoctrinate America's impressionable young into the LGBTQ lifestyle. To maintain our current population, the American birthrate must be at or above 2.0 births. Now it is at 0.73. In other words, America is dying. And the Democrats are happy about it.

We all have our impulses. We are disciplined as children to control ourselves against all impulses contrary to the word of GOD. Like it or hate it, according to the pope, the Catholic Church, and 99 percent of all mainstream Protestant religions, the LGBTQ agenda is counter to the word of GOD.

Nevertheless, a substantial majority of Christian Black men faithfully support the Democrats, a political party that pridefully advertises itself as an affront to GOD. These men are therefore involved in self-castration.

Justice Louis D. Brandeis said, "Our government teaches the whole people by its example."

Blackswithpower.com recorded:

> Now, we [Black men] engage in self-castration. Now, Black men don't have to be lynched in order to be castrated. The Society has been designed to compel Black men to castrate themselves. The Black community watches on, as a man castrates himself, and remains silent. We encourage the self-castration and then wonder why that man is ineffective. When will we stop allowing the self-mutilation of Blackness?

LGBTQ AND THE DANIEL TEST

Ezekiel 16:49: *"Look, this was the iniquity of your sister Sodom; She and her daughter had Pride."*

Jude 1:7 (KJV): *"Even as Sodom and Gomorrah, and the cities about them in like manner, giving themselves over to fornication, and going after strange flesh, are set forth for an example, suffering the vengeance of eternal fire."*

Ephesians 5:31: *"Therefore a man shall leave his father and mother and hold fast to his wife and the two shall become one flesh."*

The First Amendment: *Congress shall make no law respecting an establishment of religion, or prohibiting the free exercise thereof.*

In our Bible, it is recorded in the Book of Daniel 6:3 (NSV):

> Now Daniel so distinguished himself among the administrators and the satraps by his exceptional qualities that the king planned to set him over the whole kingdom.

At this, the administers and satraps tried to find the grounds for charges against Daniel in his conduct of government affairs, but they couldn't find anything to criticize or condemn.... Finally these men said, *"We will never find any basis for charges against this man Daniel unless it has something to do with the law of his GOD."* ...The royal administrators, prefects, satraps advisers and governors have all agreed that the king should issue an edict and enforce the decree that anyone who prays to any god or human being during the next thirty days, except to you, Your Majesty, shall be thrown into the lions' den.... So King Darius put the decree in writing.... Now when Daniel learned that the decree had been published, he went home to his upstairs room where the windows opened toward Jerusalem. Three times a day he got down on his knees and prayed, giving thanks to GOD, just as he had done before. These men went as a group and found Daniel praying and asking GOD for help. So they went to the king and spoke to him about his royal decree....Then they said to the king, "Daniel, who is one of the exiles from Judah, pays no attention to you, Your Majesty, or to the decrees you put in writing. He still prays three times a day...." So the king gave the order, and they brought Daniel and threw him into the lions' den. The king said to Daniel, "May your God, whom you serve continually, rescue you."

There was always a severe suspicion among good Christians that the goal of the Democrats in the LGBTQ movement was never about espousing equality or legalizing gay sex as most gay activists pretended. Their primary goals are identical to those of the evil men in the time of Daniel. Like them, these Democrats are facilitating the destruction of innocent people by forcing them to deny their GOD or use the government as a weapon to terrorize those who refuse to do so. It's a classic Catch-22. Either way, they win. Either way, you lose.

We have always understood that anti-Christian bigots in America who made their home in the Democrat Party are stealthily creating a society where we Christians will have to accept and fully participate in their preferred lifestyles even if these lifestyles directly violated our religious faith. If we violate our faith, we suffer separation from our GOD, thereby forfeiting his fellowship and protection. If we remain faithful, we will receive the punishment of Daniel, losing our liberty, our property, and eventually our lives. Consequently, I call these laws the Daniel Test Laws.

All our suspicions have been borne out. Democrats and their LGBTQ activist counterparts are coming to destroy freedom in America. They cannot destroy freedom unless they first destroy religion. Remember, our basic foundational understanding of freedom is based upon the fact that these freedoms are a gift from GOD and therefore irrevocable, nontransferable, and unsellable. Government is established as a servant (White Democrats owned slaves they hate serving) to assist us in preserving these rights. Assisting Americans in preserving these rights is the sole purpose of government. Without this understanding of our rights, we must consent to the Democrat Party's view that our rights are a gift from the government. Government, therefore, becomes our master. We, the people become the slave. The fulfillment of this desire fuels the entire Democrat Party. The forced compliance to the liberal LGBTQ agenda is the Democrat Party leadership's best chance at achieving this goal.

Our religion connects us to GOD. Our GOD tells us government law is secondary to his law. For the Democrat Party to have absolute control, GOD and religion must be eradicated here in America. Furthermore, this eradication must be forced upon the people. For, if the people are left to make a "decision" to surrender GOD, they may also decide to reconcile with him at some other time. But when compliance is coerced with the force of law and the gun and the prison cell to force compliance, an equal amount of force will be necessary for a correction. Man is usually too timid for such an action.

Consider this flagrant attack upon religious liberties in the clear light of day conducted by the Democrat Party: the Equality Act was passed by the United States House of Representatives on February 25, 2021, 224 to 206. All voting Democrats voted for it along with three RINO-Republicans. The text reads:

> This bill prohibits discrimination based on sex, sexual orientation, and gender identity in a wide variety of areas including public accommodations and facilities, education, federal funding, employment, housing, credit, and the jury system. Specifically, the bill defines and includes sex, sexual orientation, and gender identity among the prohibited categories of discrimination or segregation.

About the Equality Act, on May 20, 2020, gay conservative Brad Polumbo, one of the many gay Americans who do not support the anti-religion doctrine of the Democrat Party, wrote in *USA Today*:

> Its blatant disregard for basic right to religious freedom is appalling.... The bill defined "public accommodations" so loosely

> and called for regulations so sweeping that it would crush religious freedom and radically reshape American society. For example, the Equality Act undermines the 1993 Religious Freedom Restoration Act, which established a balancing test for religious freedom claims. It established a process for the litigation of discrimination, where religious employers could appeal if found responsible for an offense and their actions could be fairly evaluated. This helped ensure that reasonable invocations of religious freedom are permitted, such as a private, Catholic school only wanting to hire teachers who live in accordance with biblical values, but blatant discrimination, such as a grocery store randomly firing someone for being gay, is not. Yet in any of these situations, the so-called Equality Act would mandate that an LGBT person's claim wins by default—therefore not ensuring equality but elevating their rights over those of religious Americans. This alone is unacceptable, but the Equality Act's dysfunction doesn't stop there.

According to the Institutional Religious Freedom Alliance, the Equality Act could potentially see houses of worship and hospitals as public accommodations, thus requiring churches to provide same-sex marriages and transgender bathrooms and requiring all religious hospitals, along with all doctors and nurses, to provide sex-change operations against their will.

The Heritage Foundation says, "If adopted, the plan and the Equality Act would repeal the current administration's rule and shut down agencies that refuse to violate their deeply held beliefs."

If Democrats wanted the Equality Act passed, carving out exemptions for people of faith would be all too simple. They wouldn't demand that a Muslim be forced to sell a ham sandwich to a Black Protestant. Why would they force a Christian baker to sell a cake celebrating gay marriage to a same-sex couple? Why is the Equality Act needed? Because, to quote Utah Senator Mike Lee, "government is the official collective use of force." And Democrats are seeking the weapons of government to force Christians to obey.

The Democrats and LGBTQ activists should be ecstatic with their progress! In *Bowers v. Hardwick,* the Supreme Court in a 5-4 decision legalized gay sex in 1986. On June 26, 2015, in *Obergefell v. Hodges*, the Supreme Court decided to overrule GOD and legalize gay marriage. On September 20, 2011, President Barack Obama lifted the ban on gays serving openly in the military. Then on July 1, 2016, Obama ended the ban on transgender people serving in the military. For his efforts, on May 13, 2012, *Newsweek* magazine "outed" Barack Obama as the first gay president with a rainbow halo over his head to seal the deal. And according to Business Insider, on June 27, 2015, the US Census recorded the median income for gay couples in the United States as $115,000 per year versus $101,487 per year for straight couples. Yes, the so-called marginalized, hated, discriminated-against gay couples make more money than straight couples.

The LGBTQ activists should be ecstatic. They have everything they say they've ever wanted. So, why are they after the children, the government schools, the religious schools, small businesses, religious institutions, churches, mosques, and synagogues? They have LGBTQ equality. Why aren't they happy?

Instead of being happy, the *Washington Post* headline on March 30, 2021, said: "Dozens of LGBTQ students at Christina colleges sue the U.S. Education Dept., hoping to pressure Equality Act negotiations." The story says:

> 33 current and past students at federally funded Christian colleges and universities cited in a federal lawsuit filed Monday against the U.S. Department of Education. The suit says the religious exemption the schools are given that allow them to have discriminatory policies is unconstitutional because they receive government funding. The class-action suit, filed by the nonprofit Religious Exemption Accountability Project, references 25 schools across the country.

Understand, all these students knew and understood these colleges and universities' policies regarding sexual behavior, and they all chose to attend. Many, I'm sure, with the pretext of suing. Democrat Party leadership cares nothing for the pain and suffering in the LGBTQ community. As with Black Americans, they use LGBTQ pain for Democrat Party gain. LGBTQ is a weapon wielded by Democrats to force America into a death spiral I call the Daniel Test.

There is a tremendous amount of evidence proving that gender-reassignment surgery actually harms those on whom it is performed. Transgender adults have a prevalence of past-year suicide ideation that is nearly twelve times higher, and a prevalence of past-year suicide attempts that is about eighteen times higher, than the US general population. The US Transgender Survey (USTS), which is the largest survey of transgender people in the US to date, found that 81.7 percent of respondents reported seriously thinking about suicide in their lifetimes, while 48.3 percent had done so in the past year. In regard to suicide attempts, 40.4 percent reported attempting suicide at some point in their lifetimes, and 7.3 percent reported attempting suicide in the past year.

In a March 9, 2018, piece written for The Heritage Foundation, Dr. Ryan T. Anderson wrote:

> Sex "reassignment" doesn't work. It's impossible to "reassign" someone's sex physically, and attempting to do so doesn't produce good outcomes psychosocially.... Here's how *The Guardian* summarized the results of a review of "more than 100 follow-up studies of post-operative transsexuals" by Birmingham University's Aggressive Research Intelligence Facility:
>
> "[The Aggressive Research Intelligence Facility], which conducts reviews of health care treatments for the [National Health Service}, concludes that none of the studies provides conclusive evidence that gender reassignment is beneficial for patients. It found that most research was poorly designed, which skewed the results in favor of physically changing sex. There was no evaluation of whether other treatments, such as long-term counseling, might help transsexuals, or whether their gender confusion might lessen over time."

It is clear, the Democrat Party leadership care nothing for these children of GOD. They only want to exploit LGBTQ pain for DNC gain. Like the Black community, LGBTQ are collateral damage in the DNC war of conquest.

What is the evidence that America is currently trapped in a death spiral? On May 20, 2020, *U.S. News* reported that the Centers for Disease Control and Prevention released a study warning that "the number of babies born in the U.S. hit the lowest level in more than three decades in 2019, continuing a five-year downward trend...American women, for example, are now projected to have about 1.71 children over their lifetimes—down 1% from 2018 and below the rate of 2.1 needed to exactly replace a generation."

This death spiral started one year after Democrats on the Supreme Court legalized gay marriage against the will of the American people. Democrats have celebrated every day since the decision. Even though the Conservatives prophesied that this death spiral would occur, the Democrats will want you to believe that the timing is just a coincidence. But you're smarter than that. You cannot mock GOD. Remember Deuteronomy 30:15:

> *I call heaven and earth to record this day against you, that I have set before you life and death, blessing and cursing: therefore choose life, that both thou and thy seed may live.*

The Democrat Party is a death cult!

Now things have gotten worse. On May 5, 2021, the *Washington Post* reported:

> The birthrate in America fell 4 percent last year, marking the biggest annual decrease in decade.... It is also the largest one-year drop in births, in percentage terms, since 1965.... The fact the United States now has around 700,000 fewer births annually than it did in 2007 is much more significant, Levine said...." Losing that many people, it would be difficult to imagine that doesn't have a large effect in a broad array of dimensions."

Now, after fifty years of convincing America that the nuclear family should be dissolved, convincing women that marriage and slavery were synonymous, setting up a welfare state and a criminal justice system that systematically destroyed families, subsidizing the murder factory Planned Parenthood, and promoting the LGBTQ lifestyle, Democrats now want the government to do an about-face and incentivize pregnancy.

Indeed, on March 7, 2021, Catherine Rampell, lamenting the decline in births, wrote a column with the headline *"Opinion: The baby bust won't end without government action."* Even though the government created the "baby bust" problem, it cannot fix it. The government is only good at destroying things. Citizens fix things. The solution to the death spiral problem of America rests in the answer to an age-old mystery: Why do women risk their health, freedom, and lives to birth children, and why do men forgo their freedom, peace, and most of their wealth to get married? Both answers are "GOD." An instinct to do His will has been instilled in those who still seek Him. Democrats have worked tirelessly to separate America from GOD. This instinct of marriage, babies, and survival has likewise separated itself from much of the population. Nevertheless, Democrats still press for more abortion, euthanasia, family breakdown, drug legalization, religious repression, and LGBTQ.

We find ourselves in a death spiral whose author is the Democrat Party. The LGBTQ movement has nothing to do with equality. As a cancer and a virus, the Democrat leadership is being true to their nature. They always leave death and destruction in their wake. They have placed America and its Christians in the midst of the Daniel Test.

I trust we will pass it.

As a Black man with some experience here in America, if I could be so bold as to advise the LGBTQ community, I would recommend them not to seek affirmation from the government or strangers. Government policy and law are only a loaded gun placed to the head of your neighbors and your fellow citizens while remaining a poor substitute for persuasion and love. It is more challenging but much more rewarding and enduring. Black Americans took the road of coercion and have paid a horrible price. If you are right, you have nothing to fear. Good people will be persuaded.

Do not ask permission. Seek Jesus Christ. Seek his affirmation. Love everyone. Rid yourself of pride. Be charitable. Unless it is to defend the gospel of Jesus Christ, never intentionally offend any human being. Value your friends, forgive those who try to harm you, and choose to be happy.

CHAPTER 6:

LIE #5—ABORTION IS ALL ABOUT CHOICE

LIKE CHILD MOLESTERS, PSYCHOTICS have always existed. And in the same way child molesters are attracted to playgrounds, psychotics are attracted to abortion clinics and Democrat Party leadership. The Democrat line on abortion previously stated, "Abortion should be safe, legal, and rare." Now Democrats say abortion should be "safe, legal, and free." And even though the Democrats would kill babies for fun, it doesn't alleviate the fact that they also love to make a handsome profit from their infanticide. The Democrat Party has a unique business model where it recruits the nation's most terrible citizens, and top leadership positions are filled based upon one's level of immorality. A peculiar and sinister joy in the murder of babies results from this rampant immorality and hatred.

In this chapter, I will prove:

1. Democrat Party support for abortion has nothing to do with a woman's right to choose.

2. Abortion is championed for three reasons: an avenue to feed an insatiable blood lust, money, and pure evil.

3. Life does begin at conception.

4. Abortion is the evilest policy instituted by any government in the world.

5. The goal to make abortion illegal is laudable, but my goal is to make abortion unthinkable.

6. In the eyes of GOD, the brunt of the responsibility for this carnage will not be borne by the exploited young women but by the evil Democrat leadership that seduced them with lies.

"For you created my inmost being;
you knit me together in my mother's
womb. I praise you because I am fearfully
and wonderfully made."

—Psalm 139:13–16

"Before I formed you in the womb, I knew
you and set you apart; I appointed you a
prophet to nations."

—Jeremiah 1:5

"When Elizabeth heard Mary's greeting the
Baby leaped in her womb, and Elizabeth was
Filled with the Holy Spirit."

—Luke 1:41

Imagine the consequences when the Democrat leadership discovers they will be held accountable for abortion. Just as Democrats mistakenly believed there would be no consequences for the sin of slavery, they believe there won't be any for abortion. Evil can hide in plain sight because most people will not act to stop it. We tend to wait to see what others will do. GOD will intervene when he chooses.

In the interim, I will quickly destroy the most common and overly used abortion arguments. After reading them, you will be confronted with the profound question: Why does the Democrat Party leadership really need to legalize, finance, and encourage the murder of children? And I will answer it.

1. Lie: Life does not begin at conception.

Answer: As Democrats love to remind us, our government is secular. Because it is secular, we must answer this question scientifically not religiously. Therefore, the Oxford Dictionary definition for life is: the condition that distinguishes animals and plants from inorganic matter, including the capacity for growth, reproduction, functional activity, and continual change preceding death.

It is an absolute fact; all these attributes are present at conception.

For those who require a spiritual definition:

Job 31:15 states, "Did not he who made me in the womb make them? Did not the same one form us both within our mothers?" Galatians 1:15 says, "God who set me apart from my mother's womb and called me by his grace." And Luke 1:15, while talking about John the Baptist: "He will be great in the sight of the Lord…and he will be filled with the Holy Spirit even before he is born."

There are many more biblical verses supporting life in the womb. The argument is moot. But with their support for slavery, lynchings, rape, Black Codes, LGBTQ, and now abortion, history bears witness to one basic fact: The Democrat Party has always been led by savages. And these savages acquire power by yielding to the base elements of mankind.

2. Lie: My body, my choice.

Answer: It is illegal and immoral to use one's body to inflict harm on another or take an innocent life.

3. Lie: Government stay out of my bedroom, out of my doctor's office, and off my body.

Answer: When it comes to government schools, government education, food stamps, and so on, Democrats have always said, "Once you accept government money, you accept some government control." They have exercised this claim to ban prayer, control food purchases, and break up families in public housing.

Now, Democrats have demanded that the government pay for birth control, abortions, and all women's health in general. But demand no government interference. It doesn't work like that; you've invited us into your bedrooms, your doctor's offices, and on your bodies by accepting our money. It's simple; if you don't want our input, don't take our money.

4. Lie: Abortion is good for women's sexual equality and well-being.

Answer: After the legalization of abortion in 1973, most women's quality of life has decreased dramatically, and for most Black women, it has completely collapsed. Writing for the Catholic News Agency, Erika Bachiochi said that "abortion harms women physically, psychologically, relationally, and culturally." She cites a study in the Journal of Anxiety Disorders, which found that women who have abortions suffer a 30 percent increased risk of anxiety, depression, and suicide.

According to a 2017 report from the Samuel DuBois Cook Center on Social Equity discussed in *Black Enterprise* magazine, a single Black woman without a bachelor's degree age twenty to thirty-nine has a net worth of $0. A single Black woman without a bachelor's degree age forty to fifty-nine has a net worth between $1,000 and $2,000. According to the Center for Economic and Policy Research (CEPR) and the Hoover Institution, in 2015, only 34 percent of Black women married, down from 64 percent in the 1960s. Most sane people would consider this news catastrophic. But Democrats are proud of what they've done and are working to expand this tragedy. Why?

Democrats previously believed that abortion should be "safe, legal, and rare." But not anymore. Today the Democrat

Party platform has been amended to say abortion should be "safe, legal and free." The Ohio affiliate of NARAL Pro-Choice America tweeted, "This is a position—making abortion 'rare'—not supported by pro-choice advocates." Amelia Bonow, a cofounder of the proabortion-rights social media campaign #ShoutYourAbortion, said,

> I cannot think of a less compelling way to advocate for something than saying that it should be rare. And anyone who uses that phrase is operating from the assumption that abortion is a bad thing.

The destructive concept of forced involvement and nonrelative liability are some of the fundamental problems with the Democrats and liberalism. On April 16, 2020, Fox News reported, "Recently unsealed documents reveal Planned Parenthood charged a biospecimen company nearly $25,000 for fetal tissue and maternal blood samples in 2012." On April 20, 2016, *U.S. News* said, "A group of House Republicans presented a report Wednesday that they say shows an abortion clinic and a tissue procurement company have profited from the sale of fetal tissue." On September 12, 2019, the *Washington Examiner* stated, "In a recent preliminary hearing in the court case against the Center for Medical Progress, a Planned Parenthood official admitted to harvesting aborted fetal parts." Most of all, according to Planned Parenthood's 2014 Annual Report, they received $530 million of our money.

Democrats now force citizens who live disciplined and productive lives to subsidize the lifestyles and destructive consequences of those who hate them. There was a time when these Democrats demanded that we stay out of their bedrooms. Now they demand that we pay for their birth control, their sex-change operations, their HIV drugs, their drug rehabilitation, and their abortions, and sanction their unnatural relationships.

Real men exert their freedom, live their lives, and never ask anyone to pay for the consequences of their actions. Real men accept responsibility for everything they do and say. We do not ask the government, or the people who do not agree with us, to take care of our children, buy our guns, pay for our birth control, or sanction our relationships. We demand that we be left alone. We understand that freedom is a two-way street. If I am to be free, I must respect the freedom of others. But most importantly, in this great competitive society called the United States of America, the people of this nation must be allowed to critique the consequences of new and foreign ideas and concepts without the government propping up failure.

In business, the practice of government propping up and subsidizing failed companies is called crony capitalism. It is a destructive action. It is unfair to the consumer, who usually determines the viability of a product based on how well it conducts itself in the open market. I call the government interfering and propping up failed social actions "crony socialism." It is also a destructive action. It is unfair to society, who usually determines the viability of a social action based on how well it conducts itself in the open society. By the government supporting these actions, it generates a false positive, convincing society that fatal actions are actually good and virtuous.

Governments usually engage in these actions because the subsidized entities are either prominent supporters they must appease or enemies they seek to destroy.

Nevertheless, demanding government help and recognition is always a sign of weakness and ultimate failure. What we ultimately have is a people's contest. The Democrat Party is cannibalizing itself. We can only love them. Warn them. And get out of their way.

CHAPTER 7:

LIE #6—EDUCATION FREEDOM IS BAD; EDUCATION SLAVERY IS GOOD

PARENTAL FREEDOM HAS BEEN DISCUSSED in the United States for decades but has never really taken off. It seems to be a no-brainer. Why would a parent not want to decide how their child is educated? Democrats have said for years that parents are too stupid to make such decisions. Choice is freedom. Ergo, Democrats are saying freedom is destructive.

In this chapter, I will prove:

1. Government education is a system maintained by the Democrat Party to launder its money and pay off the unions while brainwashing the population toward socialism/atheism.

2. The nation's morality and education standards have fallen drastically with the increase in union and federal interference.

3. When it comes to failure in education, money is not the problem.

4. The Supreme Court's decreeing illegal the religious instruction in government schools has made the government education system not only wholly inadequate for Christian children and their parents but has also turned their own government into their enemy and oppressor.

5. The citizens' ability to recognize and exercise all of their unalienable rights rests upon how educated they are regarding the historical and religious origins of these rights. The government doesn't have any motivation to provide such an education. Even if it did, the courts have made it illegal, and Democrats block all effort to overturn them. Parents, however, possess every incentive.

6. The right of every parent to educate their child how they see fit is more significant than any civil or human right. It is an UNALIENABLE RIGHT given to parents by GOD. For the government to touch it without parents' absolute consent is already immoral. We must make it illegal.

"It isn't a coincidence that governments everywhere want to educate children.... If the government's propaganda can take root as children grow up, those kids will be no threat to the state apparatus. They'll fasten the chains to their own ankles."

—Llewellyn Rockwell

"You do not know the power of the Dark Side. I must obey my master." This refrain from *Return of the Jedi* was spoken by a father (Darth Vader) to his son (Luke Skywalker) as an explanation for why the father was turning his son over to the Sith (the Evil One). When I witness parents refusing freedom in education and voluntarily sending their children to schools controlled by a Sith-like organization in the Democrat Party, I am reminded of this statement. Black parents should be especially sensitive to the evil of this party.

Nevertheless, every year, most Americans in general, and Black Americans in particular, must consistently obey their master in delivering their children to the Dark Side, embodied in the Democrat Party. A healthy distrust of government is a necessity if we are to maintain a free society. A prominent indicator that we as a nation have lost our way is that almost 90 percent of American parents allow the government to educate their children and have refused any ovation regarding their liberation. H. L. Mencken once said that "the state doesn't just want to make you obey. It tries to make you want to obey." In the Black community, where distrust of government should be absolute, the converse is true. Government control in almost every aspect of their lives is virtually complete. Ironically, with all of this control, Black Americans are now further behind White Americans in education and in every other socioeconomic statistic than they were in the 1950s. Nevertheless, despite their abuse, trust in the government increases yearly and must be viewed now as a type of Stockholm syndrome accompanied by cognitive dissonance.

While witnessing how the teachers' unions disrespected parents and held them hostage by refusing to educate their children during the COVID year of 2020, it was revealed that the schools are made and run by the Democrat Party–controlled teachers' unions and not the parents. While private schools all over the nation remained opened full time, and I could not find one confirmed COVID death, Democrat-controlled teachers' unions used the fear of COVID deaths to remain closed most of the year. Because this Democrat-controlled union forbade their teachers to work, parents were forced to quit their jobs, exposing their families to extreme economic hardship. At the same time, children lost a year of education and socialization. These hardships led to depression, alcoholism, drug abuse, domestic violence, homelessness, and suicide. This all happened to parents and their children while teachers and their Democrat union handlers were paid in full.

Thus, I will say without reservation, any parent with children in the government education system who votes against any candidate offering school choice has revealed that they care more about their masters in the Democrat Party than their own children. There isn't any logical reason why any sane parent in this atmosphere would refuse the freedom of school choice. Even if the choice is to send that child back to the government school that they previously attended, choice is freedom. Having no choice is slavery. Therefore, those who say slavery cannot be a choice understand this: people voting against school choice are choosing slavery! *Democrats are saying choice is destructive; they are therefore saying freedom is destructive.*

This spirit of sacrificing one's children to a false god is biblical. Our Bible recorded that parents sacrificed their children to the Canaanite deity Moloch (also Molech or Molek). This isn't new for the Black community. They sacrificed almost all their children to the Democrat master during slavery. Today nothing has changed. Black Americans sacrifice nearly 50 percent of their children to the Democrat-controlled abortion clinics and the other 50 percent to the Democrat-controlled government school system. In Leviticus 18:21, it is written, "You shall not give any of your children to or offer them to Molech." The spirit of Moloch still exists, and it lives in the Democrat Party.

If they do not want to lose their liberty, the American people must make their peace with a fundamental concept of freedom: government education equals oppression. Amazingly, the federal, state, and local governments of this nation are conspiring to convince parents that educational freedom is bad, while simultaneously persuading them to send their children to government reeducation camps and forcing them to pay for the abuse.

Let's try something different. Let's give Christian children a Christian education. Just a thought.

CHAPTER 8:

LIE #7—RACISM IS THE PROBLEM

SINCE THE DEATH OF GEORGE FLOYD, Democrats in America have decided that racism is America's greatest problem. Is it?

In this chapter, I will prove six things:

1. Concerning ills plaguing the Black community, racism is not the problem. Black male cowardice is the problem.

2. This cowardly attitude of most Black males toward the safety and security of their family, property, and persons is necessary to maintain Democrat Party control.

3. This cowardly behavior among most Black men is a remnant of slavery and the Democrat Party plantation system.

4. Democrats know, until safety and security are established, development in the inner city is impossible. For this reason, Democrats must maintain the tradi-

tions of the old plantation system and must thwart every opportunity for Black men to establish their manhood and exercise their inalienable right to self-defense.

5. The remedy of self-defense is hidden from most Black men because history excuses Black male cowardice toward the White male and romanticizes the Black male slave as a victim and martyr. Consequently, Black men who terrorize their own neighborhoods today are glorified by Democrats and are viewed as victims and martyrs.

6. Surrendering your right to self-defense is the act of a coward. To be seen as free men and to call themselves freemen, all men must understand that the right to self-defense is not only a gift from GOD but also a responsibility. Until they know that the Democrat Party cannot protect them and decide to exercise this right and only surrender it upon death, they will always live as victims, and the entire nation will continue to suffer.

"The tree of liberty must be refreshed from time to time, with the blood of patriots and tyrants. It is it's natural manure".

—Thomas Jefferson

"Old Man Can't is dead.
I helped bury him."

—Clarence Thomas, Supreme Court Justice

On February 26, 2021, the State of Virginia declared racism a public health crisis. Since the Democrat Party controls the Black community, I guess that means that the Democrat Party is a public health crisis.

Virginia delegate Lashrecse Aird said, "It is not the same racism associated with the actions of an individual. We're talking more about Systemic Racism, that is, the barriers and challenges specifically through the lenses of race of all of our systems (education, housing, environment)."

Most Black Democrat leaders still do not attribute their freedom to GOD but to the benevolence of their former White Democrat masters or government documents. They then advance this heresy to all of America in general and to African Americans specifically. It continues to exact tremendous psychological harm to the nation. An example of this flawed thinking was on full display in the state of Virginia. On February 2, 2019, NBC News reported that Virginia's first African American Lt. Governor, a Duke- and Columbia-educated lawyer named Justin Fairfax, "carried the manumission documents for his enslaved ancestor as he took the oath of office." Fairfax said, "As I raised my right hand to take the oath of office as lieutenant governor of Virginia, I had in my breast pocket the papers that freed my three-greats-ago grandfather." This is a new kind of stupid.

Democrats say, "The government is racist." Their solution: "Let's ask the same racist government to fix racism by expanding that same racist government, increasing its ability to be racist." After 220 years, I'm sure; they'll get it right this time. These heretical attitudes are emblematic of the cowardice of most Black male Democrats and all Black Democrat politicians in America.

The Black male Democrat is aware that his people are being killed. He is also aware that it is his duty to protect them. While most Black men refuse to arm themselves, for the past 200 years they have become very prolific at begging the people who benefit and enjoy killing them to stop killing their people. It hasn't worked, but the begging continues. He is a coward. He has done nothing. Now he must pretend that he is doing something. He, therefore, retreats to his fallback position, which is racism.

This is my definitive statement: in the Black community, Black male cowardice is the problem, not racism. It is cowardice taught to Blacks by their parents, the Iron Triangle, and passed down from generation to generation. But occasionally, a flower will push through the pavement and challenge the orthodoxy of the day and do great things. One such person was Joe Frazier.

World Heavyweight Champion Joe Frazier was born in Beaufort, South Carolina, on January 12, 1944. His family worked as sharecroppers. One day when Joe was fifteen, he witnessed a White man named Jim Bellamy take off his belt and whip a twelve-year-old Black boy. When Bellamy threatened to do the same thing to Frazier, Frazier told him to keep his pants up because he wasn't going to use his belt on him. This started a chain reaction of fear from the Black men in the Frazier family, which resulted in his parents putting fifteen-year-old Joe on a bus to Philadelphia. They told Joe that he could not remain in Beaufort with them if he was going to talk to white folks like that.

Joe, however, did not take their advice. He continued to stay strong, confronting any man who challenged him. He ended up knocking out a White man, Hans Huber of Germany for the 1964 Olympic gold medal, Buster Mathis for the 1968 World Heavyweight title, and a unanimous decision against Muhammad Ali in the 1971 "Fight of the Century," handing Ali his first defeat.

This defeatist line of thinking from Black male Democrats in the South, where Blacks can kill each other but must show deference to their oppressors, led to an assembly line production of generations of Black male cowards, many of whom still sharecrop on the Democrat plantation. These so-called freemen refuse to leave, finding imaginary reasons to stay, with fear of racism being their number one reason.

Like a coward, most Black male Democrats will not compete against his master, so he must request forbearance from him in the shape of affirmative action, quotas, reparations, and other government handouts. He even relinquishes his responsibility to protect himself and his family to what has been the most violent entity in the known world for the past 200 years: the Democrat Party.

Everyone has a right to self-preservation through self-defense, the ownership of private property, religion, assembly, and speech. These rights are inalienable by GOD. I must reiterate, these rights are irrevocable, nontransferable, and unsellable. Nevertheless, the Democrat Party tells Black Americans these rights can be surrendered to the government in exchange for security. When the security inevitably does not appear, the Democrats then blame White Republican racism as the culprit. This is a lie. Racism is not the problem. Furthermore, Black Americans who believe this lie are led to slavery, poverty, and death.

Men are defined by only a few characteristics. Second to a man's ability to love is his willingness to defend because he is obligated to protect that which he loves and to provide for his family. This obligation was beaten out of most Black men by Southern Democrats during slavery. Today it is excused away and even celebrated. With a few exceptions, it saddens me to say most Black men were bred into a race of cowards; they were taught to bow, scrape, and take orders. Today, instead of admonishment by their Democrat masters, this cowardice is excused away and still viewed as a laudable trait. The Black man's inferiority is also reinforced by the fact that the slave is viewed by history as a childlike figure unable to defend himself against his godlike White master, instead of a man of free will, facing condemnation and admonishment for allowing himself and his family to be treated in such an animalist fashion.

Without retaliation and with deference, most Black men then and now allow their wives and children to be sold and abused by White male Democrats. They also learned from their White Democrat masters that this behavior toward their families is acceptable and even expected. Even today, Black men identically terrorize some Black neighborhoods with the same hatred as their Democrat Party KKK masters. Ironically, the same cowardly behavior that is frowned upon by Democrats when practiced by White Men is applauded when exercised by Black men. This cowardly behavior has become traditional in much of the Black community and has been inherited after slavery as a twisted prerequisite to Black survival. It continues to this day.

On December 31, 2020, I witnessed an interview with the great professor Angela Davis. Sadly, the substance of this interview consisted of how racism had made it impossible for Black Americans to achieve any success in America and how replacing our capitalistic system with a communist system is our only recourse. This message is parroted throughout America daily. It is now grafted into the bones of the Democrat Party and verifies the lack of discipline and immorality that they have always believed existed in Black people.

Most White Democrats are either virulent or condescending racists. Although they will deny it, Nazis, White Democrats, and most Black Democrats believe that Whites are the superior race. Therefore, Black people begging for White acceptance and placing the GOD-like power to deny or allow Black success makes perfect sense to them.

There is tremendous pain existing in the Black community. The inability of most Blacks to achieve success in America and the lies behind this failure are the cause of much of this pain. This pain cannot be quantified or dismissed, but it can be understood. This pain is a mechanism of control intentionally wielded by the Democrat Party and is intentionally left untreated. It can only be assuaged when Black people solve this one underlying mystery:

Why do most Black men participate in the destruction of their own people by surrendering the defense of their persons, family, and property to the very same Democrat Party government that has not only failed to protect them but for the past 200 years has been in charge of their abuse?

It is time for all people, but especially Black people, to eat from the Tree of Knowledge and understand that they are, in fact, *FREE*! And that they have the right, as well as the obligation, to defend this freedom with *VIOLENCE*! They must also demand that Democrats no longer violate their unalienable right to legally acquire and possess the weapons needed to inflict this defensive violence.

In the eye of the Democrat Party, slaves don't have any right to defend themselves against their master. Therefore, as they have done in the past, the Democrats will attempt to kill every Black person in America before allowing this mutiny. Accordingly, any Black American escaping the Democrat plantation better be armed.

In studying the Transcendentalists (including Ralph Waldo Emerson, Henry David Thoreau, and Theodore Parker), I found the most important aspect of life is self-reliance and independence. Racism is not the problem! Reading Socrates, John Locke, David Hume, and even the Founding Fathers—especially Thomas Jefferson, James Madison, and Patrick Henry—this concept of freedom is most important.

Everything—a high-functioning economy, religious freedom, prosperous families, moral education, and limited government—is derived from this universal concept of freedom. And freedom does not and cannot exist without an absolute belief in a law higher than government. Why would this pertinent information be excluded from the curriculum of American children in general and Black children in particular? Because this concept of freedom is always superseded by a willingness to defend oneself, one's family, and one's property with violence. Until this instinct blossoms in a man, freedom cannot exist. Therefore, the Democrat Party has pledged to obliterate this instinct within the heart of every Black American today and every American in the future.

Emerson said, "Society everywhere is in a conspiracy against the manhood of every one of its members." These essential lessons of freedom—the will, the right, and the means to execute violence to secure this freedom—are the foundation of our republic. The end of slavery in American was exacted through violence. This lesson has never been taught to most Black people. Thus, the serial rape, murder, and poverty that has never left their populace. Nonviolence, the weapon of the slave, is the only weapon afforded to them.

Furthermore, the perennial master of the Black community, the Democrats, have taught them to hate one another but to submit to the master. Democrats have never changed their plantation lesson plan of Black male castration. If they did, when did they do it?

On December 26, 1776, before his unlikely victory in the Battle of Trenton, George Washington chose the countersign "Victory or Death" for his forces who crossed the Delaware River. All his men, even Black men, were volunteers. And they all said "yes." Can cowards be free? Hell NO! Can one be prosperous without being free? No slave was ever prosperous.

Self-Reliance, written by Emerson, is one of America's most significant pieces of literature. He speaks powerfully and eloquently toward the anti-Democrat Party values that made the United States of America the most powerful country in the world: individual freedom, bravery, and self-reliance.

The Black community too often reminds me of a ten-year-old child who covets freedom and runs back when he discovers the sacrifices to maintain that freedom are more than he is willing to bear. Black men must understand that the right to freedom and self-defense are intertwined and inseparable. You cannot have one without the other. Emerson speaks of the responsibilities of freedom in *Self-Reliance*.

In it, he states:

> There is a time in every man's education when he arrives at the conviction that envy is ignorance; that imitation is suicide; that he must take himself for better, for worse, as his portion; that though the wide universe is full of good, no kernel of nourishing corn can come to him but through his toil bestowed on that plot of ground which is given to him to till. The power which resides in him is new in nature, and none but he knows what that is which he can do, nor does he know until he has tried.

Where does he speak of the alleviation of "Systemic Racism"? You cannot control how or what other people think. But you can control *you*. So, do it.

In his book *Words That Work*, author Frank Luntz asked former CNN host Larry King to pick one interview out of the thousands he had conducted; King didn't hesitate for a second.

> I was with Martin Luther King Jr., in 1961 when he was trying to integrate a hotel in Tallahassee, Florida. The hotel won't give him a room even though he has a reservation, and the police squad cars are coming because he's blocking the entrance. He knows he's going to be arrested. I'm there right next to him because I was invited there by his lawyer. So King sits down on this porch in front of this small twenty-room hotel. The owner of the hotel comes out, very straightforward but not belligerently, walks up to King

> and asks, "*What do you want?*" King says nothing, so the owner asks again in the same direct tone, "*What do you want?*" And Martin Luther King just looked up at him and said, "*My dignity.*" And that has stuck with me to this day.

I hate this story! It assumes that a White man or any man can give me my dignity. This is why liberals love Martin Luther King Jr. and the Civil Rights Movement.

Compare the Martin Luther King Jr. story with the story of Mohawk chief Joseph Brant. Joseph Brant's birth name was Thayendanegea. Later in life he took the name of his stepfather, whose last name was Brant. He was a warrior who fought with Great Britain during and after the American Revolution. For his service, Brant was presented with the opportunity to tour Great Britain. In 1785, Brant was given the privilege of being presented to King George III of England. At the presentation, everyone was instructed to take a knee and kiss the king's hand. According to George L. Marshall, Jr., Brant refused and said, "I bow to no man for I am considered a prince among my own people. But I will gladly shake your hand." However, he added he would willingly kiss the hand of the queen.

Brant understood and acted on the fact that his dignity was given to him by GOD. He refused to attribute it, or give it, to any man—not even a king. Consequently, even though, in some ways, they may be materially more impoverished and have been, in some ways, more mistreated, America doesn't have to suffer through riots, marches, murder, and mayhem by its Native American population. If Native Americans do protest, they do not protest for more government interference but to be left alone. They are not looking for their dignity or freedom. They know they already possess it.

Most of the Black people involved in the Civil Rights Movement back then and the Democrat Party now have imbued upon the government and the White man GOD-like power. They ask them for dignity, but GOD has already gifted us with dignity. No one can give it to you. You already have it. You only need to accept the gift and use it. But they do not believe it. Unlike Brant, most Blacks have been taught to ask permission. And they have never stopped asking.

This is also like the Hebrews at Sinai. During their moment of deliverance, they lost their faith, invented a false GOD, and wandered in the wilderness for forty years as a result. Most in Black America have invented and have been worshiping the false GOD of government and the White Democrat. They've made the grave mistake of not seeking affirmation and protection from one true GOD or even themselves but seeking it from an entity that cannot provide it: the government and White America. This story from Larry King is a perfect illustration of how Black America and White Democrats romanticize and glorify a flawed and failed ideology. And how most remain wandering in the wilderness of the 1960s—never learning *that when one is an heir of Jesus Christ and possesses a gun, racism is nothing more than an inconsequential thought crime.*

A racist by definition is violent, idiotic, and a fool. Nevertheless, Democrats demand that Black Americans forcibly integrate with these lower-life forms. No matter what, most Black Democrats must understand that the White man is not GOD. He cannot affirm you. He cannot give you equality. He cannot protect you. He cannot provide for you. Isn't it obvious? The problem is not racism. It is the Black community's lack of belief in themselves and their GOD.

The cure to racism:

1. Become trained and proficient in a needed skill or occupation. Race will be irrelevant. You will never be hungry or poor.

2. Whether it is Christian, Muslim, Jew, or so on, whatever your religion, practice it to the hilt.

3. Arm yourself with knowledge for the wise man and a gun for the fool.

You will then have your dignity and not have to worry about the White man giving it to you. Strength and humility, power and compassion, righteous might and forgiveness, love and protection, and honor with an absolute belief and trust in GOD, these are the qualities of men. All of us possess them.

CHAPTER 9:

LIE #8—THE BIG SWITCH OCCURRED IN 1960

IS IT TRUE THAT BLACK PEOPLE switched to the Democrat Party in 1960 and left the Republican Party because the Democrats supported civil rights and Republicans did not? Or was there another reason?

In this chapter, I will prove:

1. That the Big Switch of 1960 is a lie.

2. Instead of the Democrat Party's accepted myth that Blacks started voting for Democrats during the Civil Rights Movement in the 1960s, I will prove that most freed Blacks were voting for the Democrats in the 1870s during Reconstruction.

3. To facilitate their takeover of the party, liberals manufactured these lies to cover up the Democrat's racist past, thus duping the young people into voting for them permanently.

4. Though not perfect, of the two parties, the Conservative Republican Party policies have always been better for America in general and Black Americans particularly than Democrat Party policies.

"In the Black community, if there was an election and Jesus was the Republican, and the Devil was the Democrat, the Devil, would win in a landslide."

—Arthur Ravenel

Many people believe that the 1960–68 United States government, controlled exclusively by Democrats, was a criminal government. If you believe this, then you must believe that Democrats killed JFK and framed Lee Harvey Oswald. You must believe Democrats killed Malcolm X and framed members of the Nation of Islam. You must believe Democrats killed Martin Luther King Jr. and framed James Earl Ray. You must believe Democrats killed Robert Kennedy and framed Sirhan Sirhan. With COINTELPRO (Counterintelligence Program), Democrats between 1960–1968 weaponized the Justice Department and used it to threaten, murder, and frame mostly Black citizens.

All great criminal enterprises know how to cover up crimes and how to frame innocent people for them. The Democrat Party is no different. Therefore, after the 1965 Voting Rights Act, Democrats could no longer violate the voting rights of African Americans, and we are supposed to believe that the Democrats' racism magically disappeared after 1965. Their criminal past against Black people, previously an asset, was now a tremendous liability. How were White Democrats going to get Black people to vote for them after using assault, bribery, intimidation, and murder to keep them from voting for over one hundred years? They could not allow the Republicans to have the Black vote.

The Democrats decided to lie about their racist, violent, and murderous past. And, with the help of their friends in the press and academia, have spent the past fifty years covering it up and framing the Republicans.

Their deception has been so complete, many Black People believe Democrats freed the slaves from Republican slave masters when the converse is true.

Two of their primary, most believed, and grossest lies are the Big Switch of 1960 and the Southern Strategy of 1968. In an op-ed for the *Washington Post* on March 26, 2021, Colbert King repeated the oft-spoken falsehood that Black Americans started voting for the Democrats because of the New Deal and continued in earnest during the Civil Rights Movement of the 1960s. He wrote:

> Once returned to power, Southern Democrats state governments suppressed Black political rights—despicable actions that were aided and abetted by violence after dark. All of which deepened Republican roots in the Black community....
>
> Conditions remained that way well into the Great Depression and President Franklin D. Roosevelt's New Deal, which began to loosen the Republican Party's grip on the Black voters.
>
> But as more Black people gravitated to the Democrats, White Southerners moved with more than deliberate speed out of the Democrat Party, briefly flirting with the States' Rights Democratic Party, before landing in the Republican Party, where they are now the

> GOP's heart and soul for, in my view, all the wrong reasons: race and civil rights.

King strategically forgets to inform his reader that the Democrats have been in control of the Black community for the past 220 years. And for those 220 years, Black people have remained at the bottom of every socioeconomic statistic in America, as were Southern Whites before the arrival of the Republicans in the 1980s. After witnessing how the Democrat Party had exploited their poor White relatives and abused their Black neighbors, Southern Whites were correct to drop the Democrats. But the Stockholm syndrome of most in the Black community won't let anything get between them and their master. Today, most elite Democrats remain angry that Southern Whites caught on to their game of exploitation and racial hate. Thus, to stop the mass White exodus, White liberal elites now charge any White person who dares to defect with the sin of racism and any Black defection with the sin of being a sellout. Nevertheless, Democrats and their minions in academia, the press, and the Black community invented this lie of the Big Switch to frame Republicans for their crimes.

This lie of the Big Switch has become canon in the Black community. It is a lie that Black people only started voting for the Democrat Party after the 1960s because Democrats supported the Civil Rights Movement and Republicans. Worse than the citizens of Afghanistan placing the Taliban back in power after the Biden pulled American troops out, former Black slaves put their former White master back into power while Union soldiers were still on their soil. Culture always defeats strategy.

In her book *Five Dollars and a Pork Chop Sandwich*, author Mary Frances Berry said that her mother was most proud of the fact that she had voted "for Senator Albert Gore Sr., first elected to Congress in 1938 and to the US Senate in 1952." Gore was a racist and a segregationist. But I'm sure this Black woman voted for him solely because he was a Democrat. And that was enough. My grandfather bragged that he, like 80 percent of all Black people, had voted for Kennedy in 1960, and this was before any Democrat passed civil rights legislation. Why? White Democrats had programmed Black people to either obey or die.

Most Black people have historically sought the approval of White Democrats. From slavery until today, this pattern has not changed. It is psychological and should be expected. After 400 years of oppression, most people will eventually reflect the characteristics of their oppressor in an effort to survive.

Actually, many ex-slaves were voting for the party of their former master as far back as 1872 and were voting for them in earnest by 1876. In 1872, only two years after the Fifteenth Amendment was passed, affording Black Men the right to vote, the 1872 Electoral College map confirms that eight former slave states (Texas, Georgia, South Carolina, Tennessee, Missouri, Kentucky, Maryland, and Virginia) all voted for the Democrat candidate for president against the Union general who ended slavery: Ulysses S. Grant.

This time in history is curious. Even though the voting rights of Black Men were absolute, voting restrictions on former Confederates varied state by state during the Reconstruction era. Black men, therefore, controlled the governments of each former Confederate state, and based on our Constitution, the state legislatures decided who could and could not vote. After the Civil War, all ex-Confederates were disenfranchised and could only be granted the right to vote after specific steps were taken. The state legislatures in each individual state determined these steps.

Civil War historian and author Philip Leigh writes:

> After March 1867 Congress required that all former Confederate states except Tennessee form conventions to write new constitutions....

> Each state had to form new voter registration lists. Military occupation commanders usually selected registrars from among the minority of Southerners who opposed the region's former political leaders. Consequently, registrars eagerly registered blacks but might arbitrarily disqualify whites even when the whites claimed to have met the conditions of the Fourteenth Amendment. There was no appeal to a registrar's decision.

The Republican-controlled Congress in Washington decreed that all former Confederate states had to write new constitutions. In each state, Black men controlled these legislatures. In 2019, Leigh wrote, "By 1877, all but a handful of Confederates had regained voting rights." This means that Black men carried out the Democrat Party landslide in the South in 1876. These Black men did then exactly what their ancestors are doing now: they all voted for their oppressors. These Black men in 1876 started a tradition that has yet to be broken. Historical evidence records that ex-Confederate, former slaveholding White men were granted permission to vote by legislatures controlled by their Black ex-slaves. These ex-Confederate Democrats then voted in new state constitutions that disenfranchised Black people for the next one hundred years.

Democrats attempt to change our history by saying that civil rights were the primary concern of Black people and that this concern drove Blacks to the polls in 1960. I say that is nonsense. If civil rights were the primary concern of Blacks in 1960, they would have voted for Richard Nixon over Kennedy.

While Kennedy and Lyndon B. Johnson had not yet done anything for civil rights, Dwight D. Eisenhower and Nixon had done the following:

1. Invited Martin Luther King Jr. and those Black people involved in the Montgomery bus boycott to the White House.

2. Ordered the deployment of the 101st Airborne to enforce the court-ordered integration of Central High School in Little Rock, Arkansas (also known as the Little Rock Nine case).

3. Given the first Oval Office address (Eisenhower) on the topic of race.

4. Passed the 1957 Civil Rights Act.

5. Passed the 1960 Civil Rights Act.

The Republicans, Nixon, and Eisenhower had accomplished all this before the Democrats, Kennedy, and Johnson had done anything. Therefore, I submit, if civil rights were the driving force behind Black participation in 1960, Black Americans would have voted Republican, not Democrat.

What then has been the driving force behind the Black electorate since 1872? Stockholm syndrome and cognitive dissonance. Like their slave ancestors before them, Black Democrats continue to be so enamored with their White masters that for the past 160 years, they have gone to court, conducted sit-ins, and been beaten, jailed, bitten by dogs, shot with water hoses, and killed just to sit on the toilet or eat a hamburger beside them.

And White Democrats already suffering from White supremacy believe that it all makes perfect sense. Why wouldn't Blacks prefer White Democrats' presence and covet their lives and culture over that of their inferior people?

Because they possess the powers of GOD, why shouldn't Blacks request that White Democrats correct all that is wrong in the lives of Black America? Moreover, Black and White Democrats are so convinced of White Democrat superiority they believe that if White Democrats could only wrest the control of government away from the people, Democrats could not only save the Black community but also turn Black Democrats White.

CHAPTER 10:

LIE #9—THE CIVIL RIGHTS MOVEMENT HELPED BLACKS

DEMOCRATS DO NOT RECOGNIZE the rights of the individual. They view every individual as a member of a collective group. This group's leadership is chosen by the Democrat Party leadership and receives their instruction from them too. Whether they be Black, LGBTQ, women, or Hispanic, every member of this group is expected to conform to the tenets of the party or be punished.

When Democrat leadership speaks of gains achieved during the Civil Rights Movement, they speak from the vantage point of a plantation master. To be clear, they mean gains made for themselves, not for Black Americans. They are the masters, and when a larger-than-expected cotton crop was harvested, the plantation master viewed that year as very profitable from his vantage point. There is no correlation, however, between the Black slave's position and his White master. While the master has gotten more prosperous and more powerful, the slave is poorer and still a slave. Likewise, in the Democrat Party, while their leadership has gotten rich and powerful, the Black Democrat is still poor and admits he is still a slave.

Lincoln believed that the party's leadership was attempting to enslave every American of every race. Their poll taxes and literacy tests disenfranchised poor Whites and women along with Blacks. Lincoln was correct then, and I am correct today. The Democrat Party is evil.

Gains made during the Civil Rights Movement were positively felt mostly by liberal Whites and Black collaborators. On the aggregate, Black Americans lost ground and have been losing ground since 1965.

In this chapter, I will prove:

1. Black Americans did not gain anything from the Civil Rights Movement; they actually lost ground.

2. The destruction of the Black community via the Civil Rights Movement by the Democrats was intentional.

3. To give socialists control of one of the United States major political parties was the sole purpose of the Civil Rights Movement.

4. Democrat leadership, and their minions in the press, lied, manipulated, and destroyed the lives of millions of good people in their quest to accomplish this takeover.

5. Continuous racial animus manufactured by the Democrats is necessary for them to maintain power.

6. Before America can have real racial healing, this fake history must be revealed.

7. For many Black Americans, no amount of evidence will ever change their minds.

"For those with faith, no evidence is necessary; for those without it, no evidence will suffice."

—Thomas Aquinas

The condition of Black people today bears witness to a basic fact: the Civil Rights Movement did nothing to help Black Americans. To put it simply, the Civil Rights Movement was an orchestrated event designed by White Northeastern liberals to take over the Democrat Party by registering over three million latent Black votes located in the old South. Because of White Democrat violence and Black male cowardice, an alternative to the Democrats did not exist in the South. Northeastern White Democrats watched Black Southerners fight, bleed, and die in their attempts to drink water, use the bathroom, eat, and go to school beside racist Southern White Democrats. They correctly surmised that these Southern Blacks, if given the opportunity, would vote for these same racist White Democrats that they had held in such high esteem. Conversely, Republicans believed that no sane Black person would vote for the party of the Confederacy, Ku Klux Klan, and Jim Crow.

Republican President Eisenhower and Vice President Nixon had hosted Martin Luther King Jr. and other civil rights leaders at the White House after the Montgomery bus boycott. Eisenhower deployed the 101st Airborne to protect the Little Rock Nine in 1957, passed the 1957 Civil Rights Act after a Democrat Party filibuster, and passed the 1960 Civil Rights Act, which protected the rights of Black people so they could vote against the Democrat Party opposition. Republicans believed that when compared to the Democrat record of undeniable hatred for Blacks, Republican support for Black Americans was undeniable and believed that they had earned the Black vote.

The Republicans were wrong. Eighty percent of Southern Blacks registered to vote by the Freedom Riders, Freedom Summer, National Association for the Advancement of Colored People (NAACP), Southern Christian Leadership Conference (SCLC), Congress of Racial Equality (CORE), Student Non-Violent Coordinating Committee (SNCC), Urban League, and so on, voted for the Democrat Party. The Democrat Party then used those votes to expand their evil. The pre-1970s Democrat Party was merely a party of Black-hating racists. The post-1970s Democrat Party remained Black-hating racists but also became a death cult. They expanded their evil to include the government-funded murder of children, the destruction of the family, the repression of religious liberties, the repression of the right to self-defense, the destruction of public education, the spread of Marxism, and the enemy of everything that is good and wholesome. Exploiting the undeniable fact that most Black voters will never leave them, Democrats have used this unchecked power to celebrate the vile and grotesque while attacking the beautiful and sublime. They are a cancer. They are the walking dead. They are cannibalizing themselves. Like their father, the Devil, they are liars and murders. They are beasts that walk this world with human feet whose only aim is to kill, steal, and destroy. And they cannot survive without the support of Black Christians. Isn't that ironic?

BLACK EXPLOITATION

For every step forward in the Civil Rights Movement, Black Americans have taken two steps backward. The exact structure designed to keep Black people in line on the Democrat plantation of the Antebellum South still exists in today's Democrat Party. I call it the Iron Triangle, which as previously defined consists of most Black preachers, Black politicians, and Black civic organizers. *If any Black American has made any forward progress since 1960, it is in spite of, not because of, the Civil Rights Movement.*

The Civil Rights Movement and the DNC are attempting to take credit for an organic change in most young Black people that took place in the 1960s and '70s. These young Black people simply refused to live as their parents had lived regarding White America. There wasn't any law passed by Congress ordering Black people to stop going to the White man's back door or saying, "Yessa boss," to White men. These Black people stopped because they simply chose to stop. The law doesn't make me a slave or free. A person is a slave because they've chosen to be one. I am not a slave because I have decided not to be one. They can pass a law tomorrow saying that I am a slave, dog, or rabbit, but it will not matter. I decide who I am. But Democrats and the Civil Rights Movement have told the world that they "set" me free, and I owe them. This line of thinking is insanity. It is an anathema to freedom and Christianity. GOD gave me my freedom; no one can take from me. It is irrevocable, irreversible, and nontransferable. And anyone who says otherwise is a liar, a hypocrite, and an apostate.

Nevertheless, to be enjoyed, every gift and blessing first must be accepted. Like many other Americans, I have accepted my gift. Sadly, for the past 220 years, the Democrat Party has created a separate division in their party exclusively designed to convince Black Americans to reject GOD's gift of freedom, security, and abundance and to accept Satan's gift of slavery, poverty, and death. Most have fallen for this lie, and their broken lives are a testament to this folly. Democrats now have plans to force this evil slavery on all of America.

Many Americans still proudly recite the tired old mantra from Martin Luther King Jr.'s "I Have a Dream" speech when King says: "I have a dream that my four little children will one day live in a nation where they will not be judged by the color of their skin but by the content of their character." What is wrong with the color of my skin? One hopes not to be judged by something for which they are ashamed. For instance, you would hope not to be judged by someone if you are usually well-groomed but are seen on the day you had to run to the market in your sweats because of an emergency. You hope not to be judged when you have unexpected visitors on the day when your home is messy because you are cleaning the attic and things are everywhere. We ask not to be judged by these embarrassing situations. Black people pleading with the rest of America not to judge them by the color of their skin is an admission that something is wrong with Black skin. Because of this self-destructive belief, it is apparent in their music, their conduct, their culture, and their almost-unanimous support for the racist Democrat Party. Because they are consistently comparing themselves with White America, most of the Black community live in a state of constant self-hate. This self-hate did not start with the Civil Rights Movement, but the Civil Rights Movement cemented it into America's psyche. This flawed ideology must be pulled uprooted from stem to stern.

How is it that Black people are the only race in America that has been taught by its leaders to hate themselves? Has White, Jewish, Asian, Hispanic, or Arab leadership pleaded with America not to judge them? No! Consequently, unlike the inner city Black community, these minority groups are not currently enveloped in a fratricidal death spiral.

It saddens me tremendously whenever I hear Black Americans say or sing, "Someday we will be free." I hope one day to hear them sing and say, "Today, I know I'm free." Because "FREEDOM" is already theirs; they need only to accept it. Satan, the accuser, and his storm troopers in the Democrat Party leadership seek to keep them in bondage, incentivizing them to reject this GOD'S gift of freedom. Therefore, they needlessly suffer. Any person admitting to their slavery is submitting to Satan's hate and poverty while rejecting the love and abundance of Christ. Because "whoever the Son frees is free indeed." Waiting to be set free by men is a fool's errand and is an insult to GOD.

All races, all nations, and all people are BEAUTIFUL. Black is also beautiful. Why would I not want to be judged by something that is beautiful?

If some racist doesn't like the color of my skin or is offended by it, what kind of man would I be to let it affect me? He has the problem. Not me. I will love him and pray for him, but I will never beg for his acceptance. This mantra of self-love and self-acceptance should be the new ideology of not just Black America but all of America and the world. And the mantra of self-hatred, envy, covetousness, and pleas for approval should be buried in museums with all the other relics of the Jim Crow South.

THE PLO AND BLACK LEADERSHIP

Black leadership after the Civil Rights Movement has a better resemblance to the PLO (Palestine Liberation Organization) than any part of a democratic government built on freedom, capitalism, and free markets. Like the PLO, the Black Democrats have kept the Black community in a state of constant warfare, victimization, and poverty. And like the PLO leadership, Black politicians have supported false religion, instigated race hatred, and facilitated a dystopia among their people, all in a quest to retain power and wealth for themselves. They then take no responsibility for the failed outcomes of their leadership. Instead, they use the old scapegoat model. The PLO scapegoat the Jews, and Black Democrat leadership scapegoat America.

It is amazing to witness how two similar races of people can live in areas only miles apart, and one group can become tremendously wealthy while the other group remains tremendously poor. This phenomenon is witnessed today when we pay attention to North versus South Korea, Venezuela, and Cuba versus America, and during the Cold War, East Germany versus West Germany. Within the border of the United States, this contest is played out in real time.

In states where wealth is abundant, you will find abject poverty whenever you find clusters of primarily Black people. You will find sets of poor White people, but you will also find groups of rich White people. You very seldom find clusters of rich Black people. What is the common denominator? With nations and communities, wealth and poverty have nothing to do with color. It has everything to do with the political and economic system by which the people live.

All these poor countries live by a socialist ideology. The inner cities and majority Black congressional districts have followed suit. Why would they do this after witnessing the poverty and death that these systems create? Because these systems also create absolute power and stability for its leadership class. Crime and poverty don't matter. Black Democrats usually don't lose reelections in these socialist districts. Like the PLO, they either resign, die in office, or go to jail.

We can thank the socialism of the Civil Rights Movement for this curse.

Immediately after the inert Civil Rights Acts and Voting Rights Acts passed, the socialists/communists who had been anonymous in the movement finally decided to emerge and take control. According to David Garrow in his book *Bearing the Cross*, King was more concerned with socialist economic views than Black capitalism. Indeed, the demands of Martin Luther King Jr.'s "Poor People's Campaign" were written and devised by his communist friend Stanley Levison and read like it could have been dictated from the Red Square in Moscow. It called for $30 billion annual appropriations for the comprehensive antipoverty effort, full employment, a guaranteed annual income, and construction funds for at least 500,000 units of low-cost housing per year. This government control is the meat and potatoes of socialism and always leads to poverty and death.

THE CIVIL RIGHTS MOVEMENT WAS NOT NONVIOLENT

In the movie *The Godfather*, Vito Corleone is asked by his godson, Johnny Fontaine, to secure Johnny's release from a contract owned by a bandleader. Vito offers the bandleader $10,000 to let Johnny go. The bandleader refuses. Vito returns the next day, but this time with his enforcer Luca Brasi. The bandleader agreed to let Johnny go for $1,000 because Luca Brasi put a gun to his head and promised him that his signature or his brains would be on the contract.

Question: Was Vito Corleone a nonviolent man? Most of us would say no. If asked whether Vito Corleone a violent man, most of us would say yes. Then how can we say that the Civil Rights Movement was a nonviolent movement? Vito Corleone did not use violence to get what he wanted. He contracted Luca Brasi, a third party, to conduct violence on his behalf. This action made Vito complicit in the violence and, therefore, violent himself.

Wasn't convincing the government to pass laws threatening violence on White Americans who resisted their wishes the primary goal of Martin Luther King Jr. and the Civil Rights Movement? The goal was not to implement the edicts of Christianity by changing the hearts and minds of their enemies. The Civil Rights Movement's stated goal was to pass federal legislation designed to get what they desired. And when federal legislation is passed, the naked use of force and violence is not only implied but expected when enforced.

The Civil Rights Movement and Martin Luther King Jr. used the government as a third-party contractor to implement violence on their behalf in the same way Vito used Luca Brasi. With the government holding the barrel of a gun to the heads of racist Whites, the Civil Rights Movement forced them to allow Blacks into their schools, restaurants, and bathrooms. Today, Black Lives Matter, LGBTQ organizations, and Antifa are utilizing the same gangster tactics by using the United States government as their private enforcer. They intend to turn our government into their own private Luca Brasi. They intend to call on it whenever they desire to force the rest of us to comply with their radical demands of wealth redistribution, public school indoctrination, Critical Race Theory, gun confiscation, religious repression, and so forth.

With the government holding a gun to the head of the racist White American, the Civil Rights Movement and Martin Luther King Jr. told racist Whites, "Either Black people or your brains will be sitting at that lunch counter." How does this make the Civil Rights Movement and its leaders any different from the Godfather, Vito Corleone? Now they desire to hold a gun to heads of the entire nation. Sadly, after all his speeches about love and togetherness, in the end, Martin Luther King Jr., along with all the rest of the Civil Rights Movement, resorted to the gun. They were gangsters and remain gangsters—plain and simple.

They did not change the hearts and minds of their enemies as Jesus had. Jesus Christ never asked for the changing of a single law. Without coercion, he asked that every person examine themselves and change their own hearts. Jesus could have easily resorted to coercion. Nevertheless, he allowed everyone the right to accept or reject his teachings. Jesus understood that a man forced against his will is of the same opinion still. The leaders of the Civil Rights Movement then and now obviously do not believe in this philosophy. They believed only in power. In the end, they jettisoned the teachings of Jesus Christ. Nowadays, even the churches resort to the threat of the gun pointed at the head of every American. They demand redress sanctioned by law because they longer believe in, and therefore no longer practice, the transformative teachings of Jesus Christ.

Isn't it self-evident? The $20 trillion spent, thousands of marches, and millions of pages of legislation haven't been able to overtake the teachings of the "Carpenter from Nazareth." Furthermore, most Black preachers, teachers, and parents no longer even attempt to apply it. That is why the Civil Rights Movement has failed and will continue to fail.

On March 4, 2015, CBS News ran a story titled "Have the goals of the civil rights movement have [*sic*] been achieved?" by Sarah Dutton, Jennifer De Pinto, Anthony Salvanto, and Fred Backus, which stated: "Fifty years after the Selma to Montgomery marches, Americans see progress, but 54 percent (including 72 percent of blacks) think only some or none of the goals of Martin Luther King and the 1960s civil rights movement have been achieved." The 72 percent is more correct than they know.

What were the goals of the Civil Rights Movement? Equality, integration, an end to poverty, stronger families, safer communities, and voting?

In May 2019, UCLA and Penn State University reported that school segregation is getting worse. On June 11, 2012, the *Atlantic* magazine wrote, "Schools are more segregated today than during the late 1960s." On September 14, 2017, the *Seattle Times* had the headline, "Segregation worse in schools 60 years after *Brown v. Board of Education*." According to the Pew Research Center in 1960, the incarceration rate of Black men was 1,313 per 100,000. In 2010, the last time this information was available, it was 4,347 per 100,000.

On June 4, 2020, the *Washington Post* reported no decrease in Black and White citizens' wealth gap since 1968.

The Brookings Institution reported in 1965 that only 24 percent of Black children were born out of wedlock. In 2011, it was reported that 72 percent of Black babies were born to unwed mothers.

On December 30, 2020, the *Washington Post* reported that fifty-one cities of various sizes across the US saw an average 35 percent increase in murder from 2019 to 2020. Blacks make up 11 percent of the population but over 50 percent of all murder convictions

The Big Six—Martin Luther King Jr. (SCLC), John Lewis (SNCC), James Farmer (CORE), Roy Wilkins (NAACP), Whitney Young (Urban League), and A. Philip Randolph—made a deal with the Devil. The Devil was the liberals in the Democrat Party. These liberals were atheists, radical feminists, environmentalist wackos, antiwar activists, hippies, anarchists, and criminals. When you make a deal with the Devil, you will always lose on the back end. Look at what happened on the back end of the Civil Rights Movement.

After all the sit-ins at lunch counters and boycotts of White businesses for not hiring Blacks, we now ask Americans to support Black businesses. After all the civil rights violence and demonstrations so Blacks could attend all-White universities, now they are demanding more money for historically Black colleges and universities (HBCUs). After all the court battles and legislation so Blacks could move into all-White neighborhoods, now they are complaining about gentrification and how they are being pushed out of their all-Black neighborhoods. In an effort to confiscate guns from White Americans, Blacks have found that they've only disarmed themselves. After all the marching and demonstrating in an effort to force White police officers to protect them, Blacks now complain of over-policing and police brutality, and demand that the police be disbanded. After all the marches and demonstrations demanding housing and welfare, Blacks now want the housing projects torn down and lament how the welfare state has destroyed the Black family.

By any sane measurement, the Civil Rights Movement was an epic failure. Nevertheless, many celebrate and revere it. Why? Because the Civil Rights Movement succeeded in the only arena that mattered: the vote. And the Stockholm syndrome-driven Black vote eventually gave liberals control of the Democrat Party and along with it much control of the most powerful nation in the world.

Indeed, Yale-educated author Mary Dudziak in her book *Cold War Civil Rights* argues that the Civil Rights Movement did not help Blacks and was not intended to help Blacks. She argues that civil rights was "Cold War policy" and was focused more on image than substance. American racism was a major theme of Soviet propaganda and caused nations in Latin America, Africa, and Asia to view communism in a more positive light. America needed to convince third world and African countries that American democracy was not racist and exploited the Civil Rights Movement to conduct an image-polishing campaign. It did nothing to help Black people. But it helped America's image immensely. It is in America's interest that the Civil Rights Movement must be celebrated. It has the dual effect of convincing the world and Black Americans that Black people have made progress in America because of legislation passed in the Civil Rights Movement. Nothing is further from the truth.

To most of the Black community, however, none of this information will matter. The ability to reject nurturing information is not germane to the Black community. This is a human condition lamented by teachers as far back as Socrates.

In Plato's *The Republic*, Socrates presents the allegory of the cave. In this allegory, Socrates converses with Plato's brother Glaucon. In the conversation, Socrates asks Glaucon to imagine a scenario where prisoners have been strapped in chairs, unable move their bodies or even turn their heads since birth. Behind these prisoners, however, life goes on as usual, and for decades the prisoners can only view the shadows of these people while hearing their voices bounce off the walls of the cave.

Eventually, a single prisoner breaks his chains and garners the courage to walk out of the cave, finally witnessing the truth of the real world. He hurries back into the cave to convince his fellow prisoners of what he has seen. They refuse to believe him. Even after breaking their chains and pleading with them to turn their heads to see the truth, they refuse, still fixating on the shadows.

Socrates suggested, if brought outside, those who have been in the cave too long will turn from the pain of the sun, as those believing a lie turn from the truth.

Just as the illusions in the cave drove men to believe a lie and kept them in bondage, delusions in the history of the Civil Rights Movement have driven the Black race and the entire nation to do the same.

This lie has race relations trapped in a 1960s time warp. Democrats still encourage Blacks to believe that protest that results in rioting, looting, burning, and death can somehow teach a child to read or keep a man from being murdered.

The truth: White liberal Democrats got everything they wanted. They got 90 percent of the Black vote, 95 percent of all Black politicians collaborating with their master's party, and the opportunity to turn back all the successes of the post–World War II improvements in the Black community.

Black high schools were not monster factories. They actually educated their children. HBCUs were turning out scholars. The wage gap between Blacks and Whites was shrinking. Black families were strong. Jack Johnson won the Heavyweight Championship in 1908; afterward, the Blacks had Joe Louis, Floyd Patterson, Sonny Liston, and Muhammad Ali. Jackie Robinson integrated Major League Baseball in 1946, Fritz Pollard and Bobby

Marshall integrated the National Football League in 1920, Jesse Owens won four gold medals in 1936, and Chuck Cooper integrated the National Basketball Association in 1950. All this was done by merit. These victories happened without a single march or boycott. The Civil Rights Movement stopped the progress of Black Americans dead in its tracks.

Now, most Blacks believe nothing is possible without a government program. Democrats want to take credit for everything positive and nothing negative in the Black community. In fact, the opposite is true.

The Civil Rights Movement failed at every one of its quoted goals except for the only goal the really mattered to Democrats: electing more Democrat politicians.

Ernest Hemingway said, "There is nothing noble in being superior to your fellow man; true nobility is being superior to your former self."

These racial comparisons must stop. Being better people today than we were yesterday should be the goal of all of every person As we go forward, I hope this mantra will be remembered. And the old hatreds of envy, revenge, and racial animosity will come to an end. Wouldn't that be nice?

CHAPTER 11:

LIE #10—CIVIL RIGHTS MOVEMENT LEADERS WERE MORAL

WHEN I WAS A CHILD, my family, friends, and community revered the civil rights leaders. Their pictures hung in their homes, and their exploits were legendary. Their stature was second only to Jesus. But I always wondered, if they and their cause were so righteous, how could they have failed so miserably?

To camouflage their true intentions, Democrats have cultivated the myth of the righteous, moral, and "GOD-led" civil rights leader. The myth included the lie that the FBI was racist and hated Dr. King, and wanted to destroy the Civil Rights Movement. If that was true, why didn't they murder the NAACP and Roy Wilkins, Whitney Young and the Urban League, James Farmer and CORE, or Thurgood Marshall, Ralph Abernathy, and Andrew Young? Why would they target some and not others? I could answer that question, but it would take another book.

Nevertheless, this myth of the moral and religious civil rights leader is maintained until this day. Democrats understand that America's sins could not be laid bare by sinful men. But it was also understood that men who had sworn an oath to speak only for GOD could not be convinced to sully themselves with politics. Democrats, therefore, took advantage of something that the Black community had in abundance, the crooked Black preacher.

In this chapter, I will discuss the false righteousness and absolute immorality of some of the civil rights leaders and explore whether their epic failure in civil rights and the present dystopia of Black America was connected to their epic moral failures.

In the chapter, I will prove:

1. The most prominent civil rights leaders were not moral.

2. They were valuable to the Democrats because they were immoral.

3. Because they were immoral, their message and their movement were also immoral and bound to fail.

4. The Civil Rights Movement was a garbage-in/garbage-out movement, and the Black community cannot move forward until it makes peace with this fact.

"Never trust a man whom you know
to have acted like a scoundrel to others,
whatever friendliness he may profess to
feel towards yourself, however plausible
he may be…be sure that, the moment
he has anything to gain by so doing, he will
'throw you over.'"

—Charlie Day

What are the odds that it was mere coincidence that four of the top five people in the most prominent Black Christian civil rights organization in the world were actually extreme amoral sexual deviants, liars, and oath breakers? Or were these people being actively recruited by the immoral White liberal Democrats who supervised the Civil Rights Movement?

Mathew 7:15-20: "*Beware of false prophets, who come to you in sheep's clothing, but inwardly they are ravenous wolves. You will know them by their fruits. Do men gather grapes from thornbushes or figs from thistles? Even so, every good tree bears good fruit, but a bad tree bears bad fruit. A good tree cannot bear bad fruit, nor can a bad tree bear good fruit. Every tree that does not bear good fruit is cut down and thrown into the fire. Therefore, by their fruits, you will know them.*"

Mark 13:22: "*For false Christs and false prophets will rise and show signs and wonders to deceive, if possible, even the elect.*"

How does one identify a true prophet of GOD? It is not by words. It is not for his deeds. It is by what his words and deeds produce.

1 John 4:1–3: "*Beloved, do not believe every spirit, but test the spirits, whether they are of God: because many false prophets have gone out into the world. By this you know the Spirit of God: Every spirit that confesses that Jesus Christ has come in the flesh is of God and every spirit that does not confess that Jesus Christ has come in the flesh is not of God. And this is the spirit of the Antichrist, which you have heard was coming and is now already in the world.*"

How does one identify a true prophet of GOD? The same way you recognize a true doctor, a true teacher, or a true architect. It is not by his words. It is not by his deeds. You will know him by his fruits. You will know him by what his words and deeds produce. After all their promises of integration, equality, reparations, peace, and opportunity, what did the Civil Rights Movement actually accomplish? They sold 90 percent of the Black vote to the Democrat Party. That is it. Evidence from

Chapter 9 reveals that not only did they fail to do anything else, but 72 percent of Black Americans and 54 percent of all Americans know it.

Democrats have this tendency to place maximum value on meaningless pursuits like actions, words, and intentions while holding with less regard the most important of all, attributes and results. Democrats are notorious for being swayed by words and intentions. They do this with the Confederacy and the Civil Rights Movement. Both of these movements had lofty goals that the Democrats held dear, mainly having slaves with the Confederacy and being slaves after the Civil Rights Movement.

Civil rights leaders were, and still are, great at making speeches, making promises, and inciting violence. But when it comes to improving the lives of the people they claim to represent, without question, the fruit is quite bad. According to Jesus, if the fruit is bad, then the tree is also bad. But I do not believe any of you really understand exactly how bad.

There were many actors involved in the Civil Rights Movement. I do not have the pages to focus on all of them. There were many with the best of intentions. They were good people who marched, protested, and sacrificed. Some were jailed, some were beaten, and some were murdered so the Black community could go backward. But others benefitted immensely.

This type of postmortem should not be undertaken for the sake of gossip or revenge. This exercise is necessary only if it will be used to determine where the Black community went wrong.

Of the many immoral civil rights leaders that decided to lecture America about her morality, I will only discuss four of them. The Rev. Dr. Martin Luther King Jr., the Rev. James Bevel, Bayard Rustin, and the Rev. Jesse Jackson.

No man is perfect. We have all sinned and come up short. Should not a person's justification and license to critique and judge our immorality be based on their own morality? Do lawyers hold other lawyers accountable at the bar? Does law enforcement call fellow officers before commissions? Do banks have audits?

Men of history must stand before the commissions, audits, and bars of historians. Since these men can influence millions of people for hundreds and sometimes thousands of years, their true beliefs, motives, and fellow travelers should be revealed and discussed when new information arises. If people still decide to follow the tenets of that man of history, so be it.

Thomas Jefferson was reevaluated after Sally Hemings, Strom Thurmond was reevaluated after Essie Mae Washington-Williams, and JFK's assassination was reexamined after the Zapruder film. Historical figures including presidents George Washington, Woodrow Wilson, and Ronald Reagan are facing renewed scrutiny upon the discovery of new information. Now it is time to reevaluate the civil rights leaders.

When a man's personal frailties are so extreme that they affect millions of people in an extraordinary adverse way, they need to be divulged. When they lie to millions of unsuspecting people, hiding their true motives, these motives must be revealed. Does the truth matter? To Democrats, only the lie matters. As long as people believe the lie, they can be controlled. For Black people to finally exercise their freedom, the lie about the Civil Rights Movement and its leaders must be revealed.

Many apologists, Black and White, have claimed that the information distributed by the FBI about Martin Luther King Jr., the Black Panthers, Malcolm X, Stokely Carmichael, and others was necessitated by the theory that the FBI was racist and hated these people simply because they were Black.

Whether the FBI was guilty of the thought crime of racism, I do not know. I do know that COINTELPRO (Counter Intelligence Program) was not designed to only take down Black organizations. COINTELPRO investigated organizations and people they thought were subversive to the government of the United States. Subversive organizations and people that used other means outside of the Democrat process to foment change. These groups included White organizations like the Communist Party USA, the Ku Klux Klan, the Socialist Party of America, the Weathermen, many Black nationalists, and Hispanic, Muslim, and other non-White organizations.

Some were found to be harmless and were left alone. Others we found to be dangerous and therefore were dismantled. I don't know whether the FBI sought to destroy these Black groups and people because they were Black or because they were found to be subversive. I do know that there were many like Roy Wilkins and Thurgood Marshall of NAACP, James Farmer of CORE, and Whitney Young of the Urban League who were probably investigated but were never touched.

We must remember the political climate between 1945 and 1990. The Democrat Party–controlled public educational system refused to teach our children that communism was an ideology that forbade freedom of religion, speech, assembly, press, trial by jury, and the possession of private property. Their goal was world conquest through violent revolutions by instigating internal conflict within sovereign nations and civil wars that killed millions. The destruction of the United States of America was their stated and primary goal.

I am not speaking about right or wrong, or morality or immorality. I speak factually when I say: to be affiliated in any way with the Communist Party during this era was enough to invite anything from minimal reprisals like job loss to serious reprisals like political assassination. Anyone seriously dealing with communists in America during this time had a death wish. And the FBI and CIA weren't playing around. Many of these Black nationalists, either by ignorance or arrogance, fell into this trap and paid the ultimate price.

In his Pulitzer Prize–winning book, *Parting the Waters*, Taylor Branch wrote that "in 1956 the Communist Party in Moscow ordered their agents in the civil rights movement to establish a separate national development for Negroes modeled on the Soviet Republics." It is a known fact that communists infiltrated these organizations. Taylor Branch wrote that: "*Kennedy intimated that Stanley Levison (the #1 Communist in America and a silent partner in the SCLC with Martin Luther King)* was working on Soviet orders to weaken the United States by manipulating the civil rights movement." He said King responded with "unfathomable temerity." He also wrote that the "Kennedy Administration was warning King confidentially, but in the strongest terms to cease all contact with Levinson." King said he would do it, but he never did.

Did the FBI have a legitimate reason to investigate these organizations and people apart from the charge of racism? Were these men the moral leaders they claimed to be? Were the stated outcomes of their movement their actual true intentions? Were they blackmailed, bribed, or otherwise compromised? Keep reading. Maybe I can shed a little light on the matter.

THE REV. DR. MARTIN LUTHER KING

"Nearly all men can stand adversity,
but if you want to test a man's character,
give him power."

—Abraham Lincoln

There is an old saying, "A fish rots from the head down." As repulsive as this saying might be, it is absolutely true. If leadership does not exemplify moral behavior, likely, their followers will not. Large corporations have found this concept to be absolutely true, conducting deep, intense background checks on the entire leadership and more general checks on everyone else.

In Timothy chapter 3, the apostle Paul lists the qualities and characteristics of a leadership position in the church.

He said he was to be "above reproach, faithful to his wife, temperate, self-controlled…not given to drunkenness."

Was the Rev. Dr. Martin Luther King Jr. a moral man? Let's ask First Lady Jacqueline Kennedy. According to *Politico*, she expressed disdain for MLK. On September 9, 2001, *Politico*, reporting on a tape made by Arthur Schlesinger soon after President Kennedy's assassination, quoted Jackie Kennedy as saying she couldn't look at a picture of him "without thinking…that man's terrible." She called King a "phony" and "tricky." She said President Kennedy told her how King had arranged an orgy in a hotel during the March on Washington and spoke of him in the most derogatory terms.

Was the Rev. Martin Luther King Jr. a moral man? Let's ask MLK biographer and Pulitzer Prize winner David Garrow. According to Garrow, in December 1963, FBI wiretaps revealed that King and some of his preacher friends decided to have a sex party. Garrow writes, occasionally referencing some of the transcripts, "Staying in one of the two targeted hotel rooms was King's friend Logan Kearse, the pastor of Baltimore's Cornerstone Baptist Church and, like King, the holder of a PhD from the Boston University School of Theology. Kearse 'had brought to Washington several women "parishioners" of his church,' a newly released summary document from Sullivan's personal file on King relates, and Kearse invited King and his friends to come and meet the women. 'The group met in his room and discussed which women among the parishioners would be suitable for natural or unnatural sex acts. When one of the women protested that she did not approve of this, the Baptist minister immediately and forcibly raped her,' the typed summary states, parenthetically citing a specific FBI document (100-3-116-762) as its source. 'King looked on, laughed and offered advice,' Sullivan or one of his deputies then added in handwriting."

He also reported, "At the Willard Hotel, King and his friends' activities resumed the following evening as approximately 12 individuals 'participated in a sex orgy' which...included 'acts of degeneracy and depravity.' ...When one of the women shied away from engaging in an unnatural act, King and several of the men discussed how she was to be taught and initiated."

Garrow continued later in the article, "Stanley Levinson, a 'secret' member of the Communist Party, gave King $10,000 cash in two years, the equivalent of $87,000 today." He shared that King was often drunk and that Black baseball player Don Newcombe informed the FBI that King had fathered an illegitimate child by Dolores Evans, the wife of a sterile California dentist.

Garrow told of an orgy between MLK, the gospel singer Clara Ward, and a White prostitute named Gail. FBI Agent William Been "wrote that 'Gail stated to this investigator that "that was the worst orgy I've ever gone through,' and added that she had declined a subsequent request from Clara Ward to get together again."

Regarding the Rev. Dr. Martin Luther King Jr., Garrow wrote, "There is no question that a profoundly painful historical reckoning and reconsideration inescapably awaits."

Was the Rev. Dr. Martin Luther King Jr. a moral man? Let's ask his best friend, the Rev. Ralph Abernathy. In his book *And the Walls Came Tumbling Down*, Reverend Abernathy writes about the night of April 3, 1968, in Memphis, Tennessee, the night before MLK was assassinated.

King had just delivered his "I've Been to the Mountaintop" speech at the Mason Temple. As they were leaving the temple, this is how Ralph Abernathy describes the events of that night: "It took us a long time to tear ourselves away, but we had other plans. One version of what happened later that night has it that we went to a late dinner with Ben Hooks at his home. That is not what happened at all. The real story is a little more complicated and a little less satisfying. A friend of Martin's invited us to have steaks at her house, three of us Martin, Barnard, and Me."

Abernathy wrote that King and his friend went into a bedroom while he slept and emerged at approximately one a.m. They then drove back to the Lorraine Motel in the rain. When they arrived and entered the room of King's brother, A. D. King, Abernathy added, "There was a black woman in the room as well, a member of the Kentucky legislature, and she had clearly come to see Martin. Their relationship was a close one. Knowing someone would be with Martin, I excused myself and went off to bed.... Between seven and eight a.m., Martin came upstairs." This person has been confirmed to be Georgia Davis Powers. Before her death in 2016, she verified Abernathy's claim. She was the first person of color and the first woman elected to the Kentucky senate, serving from 1967 to 1989.

Later that morning, Abernathy describes a profanity-filled beat-down that King applied to another woman. It started with this argument:

> "Why did you hang up on Ralph like that?"
>
> "Because Ralph is a poor counselor. Instead of telling you what you really are, he tells you what you want to hear. Then when you get caught, he takes up for you."
>
> "What are you talking about?" he said.
>
> "I'm talking about Ralph," she snapped.
>
> Suddenly Martin lost his temper. "Don't you say a goddamn thing about Ralph," he shouted and knocked her across the bed.... She leapt up to fight back, and for a moment, they were

> engaged in a full-blown fight, with Martin clearly winning.

I take no pleasure in recording these events. These are the words of others. They are not mine. I could have written a book on this topic alone. But they are too painful. These lines are only the tip of the iceberg. There are volumes written exposing MLK's immorality.

Now comes the cognitive dissonance. Can you handle the truth? The truth, being painful, will cause some people to explain away anything. The question: Can a man live this type of private life and not have the deficiencies bleed into his public activities? "By their fruits, you will know them."

Sometimes fate will intervene to reveal the truth. Is there any good reason why no mention of GOD exists on the King monument in DC? GOD is mentioned on the Lincoln and Jefferson Memorials, on the Supreme Court Building, the US Capitol, our currency, and the White House. Evicting GOD from this monument is not a mistake; it is an answer. It is an acknowledgment that GOD wasn't even an afterthought in the Civil Rights Movement. It was all politics.

It seems the private and public lives were one and the same. Garbage in; garbage out.

THE REV. JAMES BEVEL

The Rev. James Bevel was a minister and was a major strategist during the Civil Rights Movement, working alongside the Rev. Dr. Martin Luther King Jr. He was also a convicted child rapist who spent time in prison for raping his daughters. As the Southern Christian Leadership Conference's director of Direct Action and Nonviolent Education, he initiated, strategized, directed, and developed SCLC's three major successes, according to his Wikipedia page: the 1963 Birmingham Children's Crusade, the 1965 Selma voting rights movement, and the 1966 Chicago open housing movement. He participated in the March on Washington and strategized the 1965 Selma to Montgomery marches, which contributed to the passage of the 1965 Voting Right Act.

According to a NBC News report on October 15, 2008, Rev. James Bevel was arrested in May 2007 on charges of incest. The accuser was one of his daughters. She was between thirteen to fifteen years old during the time of the rapes. Later three other daughters came forward and confessed that Bevel had also sexually abused them.

Information from a phone call taken during a police sting operation was presented at the trial. It recorded a conversation between Bevel and his daughter without Bevel's knowledge. During the call, Bevel's daughter asked him why he had sex with her one time in 1993 and why he wanted her to use a vaginal douche afterward. Bevel said that he had no interest in getting her pregnant. He was convicted of incest and sentenced to fifteen years in prison after three hours of deliberation on April 10, 2008.

On November 4, 2008, he received an appeal bond after being diagnosed with pancreatic cancer. He died on December 19, 2008.

I know some of you will say that all the good conducted in James Bevel's life should absolve him of these detestable deeds. To what good are you referring?

The previous chapters and the following chapter prove that most Black Americans' progress stopped with the Civil Rights Movement. Poverty, education, crime, family, and religion are all worse.

Are you noticing a pattern here? What are the odds that you would have two sexual deviants masquerading as moral men of GOD and connected as partners in a political movement that has led to a dystopia? I submit to you that the communists and liberals in the Civil Rights Movement who were sexual deviants themselves actively recruited such men. Because righteous men of GOD could not have been bribed and used as these men were; they would have led this nation to salvation through Jesus Christ and would have never sullied themselves in the filth of politics.

These liberals needed and recruited these types of Black preachers—and they were never hard to find.

THE REV. JESSE JACKSON

After all the terrible things known about the Rev. Jesse Jackson, the fact that he is still given any respect or place of honor anywhere in the world is evidence that the Democrat Party and their liberal friends in the media are some of the most immoral people walking the face of the earth.

David Garrow wrote about Jackson in *Bearing the Cross*:

> Much of the trouble stemmed from a distrust of Jackson's personal motives.... "The doubt about Jesse is what is it for, is it for Jesse or for the movement?" Stanley Levinson said to Coretta King six months later, "I know on this Martin had many deep doubts." Bevel often defended Jackson, telling King, "He's just crude cause he's young." King disagreed saying, "No, he's ambitious," and voiced his unease to close friends.... "Martin had problems with Jesse because Jesse would ask questions," but others perceived a fundamental spiritual difference between the two men. "Martin saw it in Jesse," one former SCLC executive recalled. "He used to tell Jesse, 'Jesse, you have no love.'"

Long before this Baptist preacher turned against his religion and GOD to support abortion, restrictions on religious liberties, and LGBTQ, the Rev. Jesse Jackson, another close confidant of MLK and a veteran of the Civil Rights Movement, had revealed his true colors and ambitions early in his career. In his book *And the Walls Came Tumbling Down*, the Rev. Ralph Abernathy wrote about the Rev. Jesse Jackson's conduct on the night of April 4, 1968, immediately after the assassination of Martin Luther King Jr. Abernathy writes:

> It seems that shortly after the ambulance had left, the press had on the place, camera crews and reporters, local staff and network, all eager to put someone on camera to tell the story. Jesse and Hosea had both agreed that until they knew what had happened, they would avoid the press and stay out of sight. At least that's what Hosea had thought was the understanding.
>
> So, he was more than a little surprised to look out the window and see Jesse standing in front of several cameras speaking into a microphone that a reporter was holding in his face. Curious, Hosea slipped outside and eased up behind Jesse, though on the other side of a chain-link fence.
>
> "Yes," Jesse was saying, "I was the last person he spoke to as I was cradling him in my arms."
>
> With a roar of anger Hosea started cursing and was halfway up the chain fence before one of

> the others pulled him down and held him until his anger had cooled. But Jackson had told the same story, or nearly the same, that morning on *The Today Show*.... Indeed that afternoon Jesse appeared before the Chicago City Council wearing a blood-stained shirt and saying that it was the same shirt, he had been wearing the previous evening when he held Martin. On June 23, 1987, the *Washington Post* confirmed the story.

On February 27, 1984, the *New York Times* reported, "Jesse Jackson acknowledged tonight that he used the word 'Hymie' in a private conversation to refer to Jews...." The *Washington Post* reported that Jackson also referred to New York City as "Hymietown." "Hymie" is an anti-Semitic slur.

On January 18, 2001, ABC News reported, that in order "to pre-empt a tabloid newspaper report, the Rev. Jesse Jackson this morning released a statement admitting he had an extramarital affair that resulted in a daughter who is now 20 months old." The married Jackson was fifty-nine, and the young lady, Karin Stanford, was a thirty-nine-year-old staffer working for him.

On July 17, 2008, the *Telegraph* (UK) reported: "Jesse Jackson, the veteran civil rights activist, has been forced to issue a groveling apology to Senator Barack Obama after it emerged he has used the word 'niggers' while disparaging the Democratic presidential candidate.... The Rev. Jackson had already said sorry for saying of Mr. Obama that he would like to 'cut off his nuts' for talking down to black people."

Even though some may try to explain away Jackson's racism, anti-Semitism, grossness, and infidelity as minor or major, his actions after King's assassination are another matter. They revealed a type of sinister Machiavellian evil that is rare in this world. His actions were so dark it has caused people like Steve Cokely and William Pepper to accuse Jackson of being an FBI informant involved in King's assassination.

To lie to the world about the murder of your friend and mentor is bad enough. But going through the labor of producing a shirt with fake blood as a prop and then claiming that the blood on that shirt is the blood of a friend who had been dead for less than twenty-four hours, all in a quest to usurp power, is a type of depravity in character only seen among the worst men in the annals of history.

BAYARD RUSTIN

Bayard Rustin was involved with the activities of the Civil Rights Movement alongside Rev. Dr. Martin Luther King Jr. longer than anyone except Ralph Abernathy. He was also a registered sex offender and an avowed and known former Communist with Communist affiliations. According to David Garrow, Rustin's activities started with organizing the Montgomery bus boycott in 1956. He basically wrote the charter to Martin Luther King Jr.'s organization, the Southern Christian Leadership Conference, and was the mastermind behind the 1963 March on Washington.

According to a story posted by CNN on February 5, 2020, Rustin was arrested in Pasadena, California, in 1953, on a "morals charge" for having sex with men. According to a June 26, 2018, article by A. Miller on the Making Queer History website, he was having sex with two White men in a parked car. He served fifty days in jail and was registered as a sex offender. David Garrow affirms this story. Obviously, this made him quite attractive to King and the leaders of the Civil Rights Movement. He was one of them.

According to David Garrow in *Bearing the Cross*, in 1957 Rustin introduced King to the number one Communist in

America and the top fundraiser for the Communist Party, Stanley D. Levinson. Afterward, Levinson took an active role in organizing, running, and financing the SCLC until King's death. This relationship between MLK, Rustin, Levinson, and the Civil Rights Movement must be taken in context. The Russian Communists had ordered the American Communists to infiltrate the movement with the goal of creating a separate national development for American Negroes, modeled after the Soviet Union, according to two sources, Garrow and Taylor Branch in *Parting the Waters*. Branch also wrote that Burke Marshall, the head of the Civil Rights Division of the US Department of Justice during the Kennedy administration, told King in 1963 that "this was not paranoid mush, he said but hard intelligence from the very pinnacle of the U.S. government." Levinson was something much more dangerous than an old New York radical; he was a paid agent of the Soviet Communist apparatus and had planted Jack O'Dell inside the SCLC to influence the Civil Rights Movement. It looks like they succeeded in their plan to make the Black people in America a model of the old Soviet Union.

President Kennedy personally told King that Levinson was working on Soviet orders to weaken the United States by manipulating the Civil Rights Movement. O'Dell was the number five Communist in the United States. With all of this information, Levinson and O'Dell worked closely and mostly secretively for Martin Luther King Jr. and the SCLC until King's death.

It is recorded that King became so dependent on Rustin and Levinson that when President Kennedy told him of Levinson's Communist affiliations and how they could scuttle the whole movement, demanding that he drop all contact with Levinson, King lied to the president and continued to see Levinson, which prompted the notorious FBI wiretaps that revealed all his indiscretions.

Bayard Rustin introduced the communist, atheist, and LGBTQ influences into what had been a pro-American and Christian Civil Rights Movement. But it cannot be forgotten, Martin Luther King Jr. could have shown the door to Rustin, Levinson, and all those malcontents. He was warned of their plans by President John F. Kennedy, who demanded that he get rid of them. But King, at great risk to Black Americans, the nation, and himself, not only kept them around, but welcomed them. Why?

Sadly, this environment of immorality and betrayal was not the exception—it was the rule. FBI files reveal many Black stalwarts of the Civil Rights Movement were shady characters. On December 2, 1996, and December 4, 1996, the *New York Times* revealed FBI files showing that, for many years, Thurgood Marshall, the NAACP lawyer who won *Brown v. Board of Education* and the first Black Supreme Court justice, was an FBI informant. Yes, Thurgood Marshall was ratting out other Black people in the Civil Rights Movement to J. Edgar Hoover.

On April 8, 2014, *Time* magazine revealed that the Rev. Al Sharpton, a Democrat operative and civil rights agitator, became a mob informant for the FBI after being compromised in an illegal drug sting. Sharpton's racism and anti-Semitism are well documented, but because of his immortality—not in spite of it—he has been recruited by the Democrat Party and is a pivotal player in their politics.

Criminals, deviants, and informants exist throughout "moral" civil rights and Black political leadership then and now. Actually, it would be difficult not to find one who isn't. Could this be a coincidence or the simple law of attraction: "We attract what we exude"? Or was this the Black Democrat leadership model? Indeed, in the book *Bearing the Cross*, MLK's friend, colleague, atheist, and socialist Michael Harrington, was quoted as saying about the Civil Rights Movement, "this was not a sour-faced, pietistic endeavor. Everybody was out getting laid."

The Civil Rights Movement was an immoral product of communism, Black inferiority, and Black government dependency that could only be sold by an immoral group of Black leaders, which eventually led to immoral outcomes. One fact is irrefutable: for the Black community, most progress stopped when this pack of weirdos and deviants took over. Sadly, most Black Americans are still so brainwashed; instead of lamenting these relics as failures, they revere them as heroes.

We know this rotten fruit by its rotten tree.

CHAPTER 12:

LIE #11—WHITE PRIVILEGE, CRITICAL RACE THEORY, AND SYSTEMIC RACISM SHOULD BE TAKEN SERIOUSLY

HOW CAN ONE BE A CHRISTIAN and believe that anyone has privilege over you or that you can be oppressed? Yet most Black Democrats, 85 percent who profess to be Christian, believe in White Privilege. What is White Privilege? Racism.org defines it as:

a. A right, advantage, or immunity granted to or enjoyed by White persons beyond the common advantage of all others; an exemption in many particular cases from certain burdens or liabilities.

b. A special advantage or benefit of White persons; with reference to divine dispensations, natural advantages, gifts of fortune, genetic endowments, social relations, etc.

Institutional racism is defined as a form of racism that is embedded as a normal practice within society or an organization. It can lead to such issues as discrimination in criminal justice, employment, housing, health care, political power, and education, among other issues.

Our Bible consistently reminds us that GOD blesses, loves, and protects us.

How can any Christian believe in White Privilege? GOD loves all his children equally. He knows your name. No matter what they tell you, you must believe it.

When you believe it, you become bulletproof.

In this chapter, I will prove five things:

1. White Privilege and Systemic Racism are lies devised by the Democrats as mechanisms to continue the Black slave mentality that believes only White America, not GOD, has the power to infuse Blacks with dignity and self-respect. Therefore, this makes the White man GOD in their eyes.

2. White Privilege and Systemic Racism are lies designed to convince Blacks that Whites are superior and have the ability to control all outcomes regarding their lives.

3. White Privilege and Systemic Racism are lies designed to convince Blacks that they cannot succeed in America no matter how hard they try.

4. White Privilege and Systemic Racism prove that the Black preacher, Black civic organizer, and Black politician are failing the Black community but giving the Democrats everything they want.

5. "Critical Race Theory" is a Democrat Party scheme designed to produce the same self-hatred and inferi-

ority complex in the White community that they've instilled in most of the Black community and used to maintain control over it.

"What are human beings that you should notice them, mere mortals that you should think about them? For they are like a passing shadow."

—Psalm 144:3-4

"Excellence Negates Racism. It also negates biases in national origin, gender, color, height, weight, or any other excuse you may want to use."

—Vince Everett Ellison

White Privilege is a lie. I am a Black man. No White person has privilege over me. Black people who believe in White Privilege are slaves looking for masters, and White people who believe it are masters looking for slaves. The reason for most Black American dysfunction is the fact that too many of them believe the lie that another race has privilege over them. This mindset is a recipe for failure.

The implementation of Critical Race Theory in public education is a veiled attempt by Democrats to teach White people to hate themselves, the same way they've taught most Black Democrats to hate themselves. Critical Race Theory will indoctrinate White people into a state of victimization where they murder, rape, oppress, and destroy one another. In most of the Black community, it has worked tremendously well. White parents should fight this at all costs. If Democrats succeed, all of America will be a ghetto.

Democrats succeed when populations feel that they are not worthy of freedom. Democrats thrive when people are convinced that the challenges of liberty are insurmountable and their survival rests in the comfortable arms of enslavement.

The dysfunction of the inner cities can be traced to this phenomenon. Its success has afforded the Democrats absolute control, and they intend to expand it. Critical Race Theory is the vehicle they intend to ride to this destination. White America beware.

As a young man, I was a part of my family's gospel singing group, "The Ellison Family." My mother and father sang this incredible duet entitled "I Wonder Is the Lord Satisfied with Me?" It was a hit all over the South. It also asked the most pertinent question. We Christians should only be concerned with that one question. Nevertheless, Black Democrats who believe in White Privilege and Systemic Racism ask, "I wonder is White America satisfied with me?"

Black people are too concerned with how White people feel about them. Worrying about how one is viewed by man is self-destructive. The Black community's current condition confirms that theory. Black Americans should be concerned only with our conduct. If they hate us, we love them. If they discriminate against us, we treat them fairly. If they lie about us, we tell the truth about them. This is how we protect ourselves and affirm our relationship with GOD. And as a complimentary prize, we will convert the racist and assist in saving their soul.

From Muhammad Ali screaming, "I am the Greatest," to James Brown singing. "Say It Loud—I'm Black and I'm Proud," everything Black Americans have learned for the past fifty years is now being jettisoned for one reason: Black American belief in their equality or superiority to White Americans is the death knell to the Democrat Party. The solution: take back your power. As a Black man, it is an insult for anyone to insinuate that any man, Black or White, has any privilege over me. As a Christian, it's blasphemy.

You cannot believe in White Privilege and be a good Christian. It is a fact that most of the promoters of this false belief, Ta-Nehisi Coates, George Soros, the founders of Black Lives Matter, and most of the Democrat Party leadership, have been reported to be atheists. But all of this matches. In my first book, *The Iron Triangle*, I discussed how most Black preachers, Black civic leaders, and Black politicians had formed an Iron Triangle and are paid to keep Black Americans dependent on the Democrat Party. The sad fact that White Privilege is not being laughed out of existence by many Black people is a testament to the success of the Iron Triangle in keeping the Black community on the Democrat Plantation.

For centuries Black Americans only requested a chance to try. In the NFL, MLB, or NBA, or at Harvard or IBM, we only asked for the opportunity to try. If we were not good enough, it only meant that we hadn't found our talent—nothing else.

If your race can be used as a reason to not employ or promote you, this is probably a job that you do not want. Legally forcing such people to surrender employment under threat of imprisonment is never beneficial to the person hired. The fact that this employer will be bankrupt soon should be reason enough. Think about a sports team that has decided it doesn't want Black athletes. That team's racism will cause it to become uncompetitive, as any high-quality business would, and it will die as a result.

Companies that refuse great talent due to race are stupid and are therefore insolvent. But, if you have no skills and no work ethic, racism can be used to deny you employment, and you will not be missed.

When you decided to be average or, GOD help you, below average, you have conceded to every antagonist the license to use race, gender, national origin, height, weight, and so on, as a determining factor. No sane employer or person would cut their own throat by dismissing an individual who adds value to their company or their lives based on melanin content. Therefore, you will find that accusations of White Privilege and Systemic Racism are hurled by those who are average or below average in the endeavor they have chosen to pursue. Instead of improving their faults, they take refuge in an old, weak, and unprovable argument and scream that they were denied either because of White Privilege, Systemic Racism, or some other prejudice. Afterward, they feel so much better, while the faults that have plagued their development remain an impediment.

Real power will come when every individual Black person does what every successful person has done and conduct a personal assessment, understanding what they may lack or possess in knowledge, appearance, and manner that may help or hinder their desired pursuits. Then have the courage and discipline to correct it.

Here is the real truth; a truth that Democrats will hide from Black America and all of America and will die before they reveal it. There are three rules to personal and economic success in America. None of them include being White. Educate yourself. Work hard. Believe in GOD. Then as Henry David Thoreau wrote in *Walden: "WALK CONFIDENTLY IN THE DIRECTIONS OF YOUR DREAMS!"*

CHAPTER 13:

LIE #12—DEMOCRATS DON'T STEAL ELECTIONS

THE ELECTION OF 2020 will go down as the most tumultuous election since Abraham Lincoln's in 1860. With impeachment, racial violence, a global pandemic, and national depression as the backdrop, President Donald Trump's claim that the Democrats stole the election led to an insurrection and the storming of the United States Capitol.

The mainstream press and liberal media reported that his claims of election stealing were not only unfounded but also impossible. In this chapter, instead of concentrating on the 2020 elections, we will explore the Democrat Party history of stealing elections.

In this chapter, I will prove:

1. The Democrats have been stealing elections since 1870.

2. Democrats started using bribes, intimidation, and ballot stuffing to control the Black vote and the Black community.

3. Bribes, intimidation, and ballot stuffing to control the Black inner cities and congressional districts are tailor-made for this chicanery.

4. Democrats have always used and activated paramilitary organizations in their quest to steal elections.

5. Democrats would lose most of their power if they did not steal elections.

"If you ain't cheatin' you ain't tryin'."

—Al Davis, Oakland Raiders

I am sure the Democrat Party was saying this one hundred years before Al Davis. The Democrat Party's ability to steal elections is legendary. Stealing elections is now grafted into their culture. They steal votes even when they don't have to steal. As a matter of fact, Democrats would prefer to steal an election than win it legally.

"Keep the Nigger down and the of cost of cotton up" was the slogan of US Senator Ellison DuRant "Cotton Ed" Smith, a Democrat from South Carolina. He served from 1909 to 1944. He screamed the slogan from the mountaintops while Black people labored in his cotton fields. Remember Faulkner: "The past is never dead. It's not even past." Blacks still struggle in the same poverty and oppression as in 1944. In the ghettos of the inner cities and the majority-Black districts of the Democrat Party, although unspoken, the Democrat slogan is still the same as Cotton Ed's in 1944, except for four words. Now it's "Keep the African Americans down, and the vote count up." We are to believe that all this intraparty racism mysteriously disappeared after 1965. It didn't.

How did election thievery become part of the Democrat Party culture? Let's go back approximately 150 years to 1870. The Democrats' world had officially and literally come to an end. They were living in their worst nightmare. They had lost the Civil War five years earlier. Because of the Thirteenth Amendment, they had legally lost all their slaves. Most of their property had been either destroyed or confiscated. Two-hundred and fifty-eight thousand Confederates had died in the war. The Fourteenth Amendment had given their former slaves "equal protection under the law."

Now the killer blow. With most ex-Confederates still unable to vote and Black Americans outnumbering them in many areas, the Fifteenth Amendment had granted Black men the right to vote. And tens of thousands of Union soldiers occupying the South were thwarting the ability of the racist White Democrats to do anything about it. Ex-slave Black men controlled the old Confederacy, and the white Democrat master was now the slave.

Having previously been some of the richest and most waited-on people in the world, the White Democrats were now desperate. Their darkest nightmare had come true: their former slaves had become their masters. This revolution had not occurred through any industry, risk, or sacrifice by the former Black slaves who now wished to rule over them. Conversely, many had worked and even fought to maintain the very Confederacy they had held in contempt. White Democrats understood that they had only one small window of time to act, and it was closing fast.

With this backdrop, we find the election of 1876. For the Republicans was Rutherford B. Hayes: a lawyer who had defended fugitive slaves during the antebellum years, a Union general who was seriously wounded and fought for the duration of the Civil War, and the governor of Ohio. For the Democrats was Samuel J. Tilden, the governor of New York.

Since 1860, the electoral map of the Northern, and now the former Union, states had voted Republican. The South (now the former Confederate states) had remained staunchly Democratic until Black men, with the protection of federal soldiers, started voting. In the elections of 1868 and 1872, seven former Confederate and border states voted Republican: the party of Abraham Lincoln.

Former slaves were being elected to office. Former slaves were learning to read. Former slaves were buying property. But most former slaves were still cowards and wanted federal troops to protect them from their former masters. Never mind that the Freedman's Bureau and the Union Army had given all freed slaves guns and 258,000 young White masters did not return and many who did return had lost a limb or an eye. Furthermore, the Confederate Democrats knew most former Black slaves did not fight for the freedom they were now enjoying and, in their eyes, had not earned the privileged station they now possessed. This contempt only broadened in the breast of the Confederate Democrats when most freed slaves even refused to defend their own freedom and begged for the protection of the Yankees who had destroyed the Democrats' way of life.

The election of 1876 was the Democrats' chance. Since slavery was no longer an issue, Democrats cared little for national elections. They understood that all politics were local. To hell with the White House. Democrat Confederates were going to use the presidential election of 1876 as leverage to retake their cities, counties, and states. It was going to get rough. And the freed slaves were going to understand why their decision to trust federal troops with their security more than themselves was a fatal mistake. Confederate revenge would come in an election-stealing scheme called the Mississippi Plan. This plan was so successful that Democrats still utilize it today.

Lexico.com defines the Mississippi Plan as "the plan adopted by the Democratic Party in Mississippi in 1875, of assuring the political supremacy of white people over black, chiefly by preventing black people from voting, often by the use of intimidation and violence." To end election violence and ensure that freedmen were excluded from politics, the Democrat-dominated state legislature passed a new constitution in 1890 that effectively disenfranchised and disarmed most Blacks by erecting barriers against registering to vote and owning firearms. Terrorism and fraud were used as tools of voter disenfranchisement, and to this day, they continue. This plan was so successful it was adopted by all the former Confederate states.

This plan was first utilized in the election of 1876. As previously discussed, newly enfranchised freedmen trended South Republican during the elections of 1868 and 1872, but in 1876, after the Mississippi Plan was introduced, the entire South mysteriously went Democrat, giving the presidential election of 1876 to Tilden. The election of 1876 was their first stolen election. This was only the beginning. The Republicans smelled a rat.

Immediately after the election, the Republican-controlled Congress sent a fifteen-member electoral commission to settle the question. The commission uncovered tales of murder and violence. They found that Democrats were stamping Democrat ballots with the picture of Abraham Lincoln and stamping the picture of the donkey, their party symbol, on the ballot of Republicans to fool illiterate freedmen. But the most flagrantly obvious evidence of fraud was found in South Carolina, where an impossible 101 percent of all eligible voters had their votes counted.

Voter fraud being absolutely obvious, the commission was ready to award the election to Hayes. South Carolina threatened to restart the Civil War if they did. A compromise was reached. If South Carolina seceded its electoral college votes to Hayes, among other things, Hayes would give the Black freedmen and White Confederates what they wanted. He would end Reconstruction by pulling all federal soldiers, who had been there twelve years, out of the South. Since most Blacks down South had voted for their former Democrat masters against their Republican liberators, I am sure President Hayes was relieved to send thousands of Union soldiers back to their homes and allow Black slaves and White Democrat masters to reconcile. They haven't spent a day apart since.

South Carolina agreed. Reconstruction ended. And wielding the power handed to them by Black men, White Democrats brazenly stole every election for almost 160 years, mainly by disenfranchising Blacks. Currently, Democrats steal elections by exploiting Blacks.

The entire Civil Rights Movement was necessitated mainly because of this intricate and intense motivation by Democrats to keep Black Americans from voting. When they could no longer use their power to keep Black Americans from voting, they decided to utilize the same tactics of intimidation, bribes, and ballot manipulation to control the vote.

Now we are asked to believe that Black Americans vote to disarm themselves, vote against parental choice in education, vote against keeping dangerous illegal aliens out of their neighborhoods, vote against freedom of religion, vote against keeping their babies alive, and vote against prosperity. No. Their votes are being acquired or repressed by fraud. Democrats are buying, changing, destroying, and manufacturing votes through street money, Souls to the Polls, and ballot harvesting. I could write ten books on that subject alone.

Regarding Democrats and their perennial electoral cheating, Mary Frances Berry in her book *Five Dollars and a Pork Chop Sandwich* wrote about the 2000 election in the state of Louisiana and the findings of voter fraud by detective Greg Malveaux after talking to an elderly Black woman following a complaint:

> Malveaux's respectful manner erased her doubts. She was pleased to see a black man in such a big government job. She told him she voted and began casually explaining how

> politicians bought votes on Election Day. She would be driven to the polls with instructions on whom to vote for. When she cast her ballot, the driver gave her five dollars. She didn't know this was illegal. "This is the way it's s'posed to be," she said. That was the way it was always done, and "besides we poor people need the money."…Vote buyers in rural areas acting as middlemen, generally received ten dollars per voter from a candidate who had no personal contact with the voters in the process. Half of the money, five dollars, went to the voter, as the elderly woman had told him. Sometimes the payment was "lagniappe": a pork chop sandwich and a cold drink. In urban area the process and payoffs were handled by organizations with benign names.… Local prosecutors, because they too were elected, refused to abolish the system by prosecuting the people they themselves sometimes "hired" to win office.

In the November 21, 1993 *Newsweek*, "Walking-Around Money: A Dubious Tradition" says:

> Mention money in politics and most Americans think of costly TV ads, PACs.… But the most basic—and corrupt—form of money in politics is at street level and is as old as the republic: cash doled out on Election Day.… Though outright vote buying never took hold in suburban America, it survives.… In big cities, much of the cash comes from Democrats and tends to end up in the black community.

This obscene conduct verifies every racist stereotype thrown at Black people by the people who screamed that we were too inferior to vote. Voting is a privilege, not a right. Do people who hold their voting privileges so cheap deserve them?

Democrats have never stopped cheating because too many Black voters have been willing to be bought or intimidated. It is now a tradition. Democrats cannot win without cheating. If Democrats didn't steal the election of 2020, it would be the first one they didn't steal.

CHAPTER 14:

LIE #13—DEMOCRAT LEADERSHIP BELIEVES IN GOD

A BELIEF IN GOD IS NECESSARY for the United States to survive. Our nation's founding document, the Declaration of Independence, clearly states that our rights were granted to us by our creator. Founding Father John Adams said, "Our Constitution was made only for a moral and religious People. It is wholly inadequate to the government of any other." Nevertheless, there are those in American society who have gravitated to the top of the Democrat Party who do not believe in GOD and are also attempting to create a United States where worshiping Him can land you in jail.

Consequently, policies advocated by some of the Democrats' most prominent members and the party itself have caused many to question whether the Democrat Party is openly hostile to GOD.

In this chapter, I will prove:

1. It is the objective of the Democrat Party leadership to somehow drive GOD from the face of the earth.

2. Democrat leadership will never admit to their atheism and theophobia.

3. Democrat Party leaders are socialist.

4. GOD must die for socialism to live.

"The fool says in his heart
'There is no GOD.'"

—Psalm 14:1

"A Black person voting for a Democrat
Is like a chicken voting for Colonel Sanders."

—Unknown

Many of these current Democrats and their ancestors actually burned the Christian symbol of the cross as members of the Ku Klux Klan. Democrats hijacked this symbol of peace and love and repurposed it as a sign of hatred, racism, terror, and murder. We have a better understanding of their actions on September 12, 2012. On that date, the headline in the *Washington Post* read, "Democrats under fire for removing 'God' from party platform." The story began, "The word 'God' is nowhere to be found in the Democratic national platform this year." After reading through the party platform, the party noticed that they had left out a minor individual named GOD. Someone caught it and suggested that it be repaired. But they had to take it to the floor for a voice vote. When asked for "yeas" and "nays," Los Angeles Mayor Antonio Villaraigosa clearly heard that the "nays" massively outweighed the "yeas." Yes, you read correctly: a vast majority of the Democrat Party leadership voted to leave GOD out of its party platform in front of the world.

Looking embarrassed and panicked, Villaraigosa looked behind the stage curtain for guidance. He got an answer. He yelled into the microphone, "The Yeas Have It!" Villaraigosa was booed off the stage.

The shameless repudiation of the Almighty in front of the entire world was the Democrat Party's atheist-coming-out party. It had been conventional wisdom for over 220 years of American government that any political party that outwardly promoted atheism was dead. Villaraigosa did save them. But by shamelessly lying about the vote, he simultaneously saved the Democrats and validated everything that I already knew about them: Democrat leadership is evil. It is atheist. And they get away with it because they lie.

This confession did not affect the so-called Black preachers who sulk their way through the party. If abortion and LGBTQ have not caused them to bolt, the endorsement of Satan himself will not cause these slaves to leave their master. Their quest to erase GOD from the face of the earth is relentless and unyielding. On March 17, 2021, the *Washington Post* described the Equality Act that passed with a unanimous vote from the Democrat-controlled Congress:

> What makes it more sweeping that past anti-discrimination measures is it explicitly overrides the Religious Freedom Restoration Act (RFRA), which prohibits the federal government from "substantially burdening" individuals' exercise of religion unless it is for a "compelling government interest."
>
> While enacted in 1993 with overwhelming bipartisan support, the RFRA in recent years has been most loudly championed by

> social conservatives. LGBTA and civil liberties advocates say the RFRA has been used to allow discrimination.

Ergo: Democrats believe that some practices of Christianity are discriminatory and therefore should be illegal. Two Thessalonians 2:11–12 speaks of this insanity. It reads, "And for this cause GOD shall send them strong delusion, that they should believe a lie: That they all might be damned who believed not the truth, but had pleasure in unrighteousness."

A belief in GOD is a necessity for a human being to even understand the origin and concept of freedom. Much of our contemporary concept of freedom derives from John Locke's *Second Treatise of Government.* Locke believed:

> From the presumed intention of GOD it followed that men were naturally equal in the sense that no-one had more power or jurisdiction than another, and were naturally free "to order their actions, and dispose of their possessions and persons, as they think fit, within the bounds of the law of nature" which forbids anyone harming another or destroying himself, and requires each to try "when his own preservation comes not in competition" to preserve the rest of mankind.

Our unalienable rights come from GOD. According to the founding document of our republic, the *Declaration of Independence*, government is instituted by men to help secure these rights and should be abolished when it refuses to assist or when it becomes a violator of these rights. If GOD does not exist, our whole concept of a nation is a lie and has no foundation. Democrats know this, and this is their plan.

Since Democrat Party leadership does not believe in GOD, they do not believe in America. Since their support for slavery, Jim Crow, and now abortion, it is apparent that they believe in something totally different and always have. If our rights do not come from GOD, from where do they come? They either come from the individual—this will make every person a law unto themselves—or they come from the government—this is Marxism or Communism. In this form of government, unalienable rights do not exist, only the power of the state. Sound familiar?

To make it simple: no GOD; no America. This is the Democrat Party end game.

Everything about Christianity is an anathema to the Democrat Party. The Democrat Party is primarily a party of grievance, lies, murder, and nonaccountability. Democrat Party members demand reparations for someone else's slave labor. Democrat Party members believe that they should be allowed to take money from their neighbors. Democrat Party members believe that because their children are inconvenient, they should be able to murder them. Democrat Party members believe that they should be able to disarm their neighbors, leaving them vulnerable to the predators of society. Democrat Party members believe that they should be able to censor, punish, intimidate, and hurt people with whom they disagree. Democrats believe that government should provide your children with a secular Hollywood education.

Conversely, Christianity believes in forgiveness instead of reparations. Christianity believes that GOD, not government, will fulfill our needs. Christians believe in love and life, not abortion. Christians believe that GOD has blessed us with our possessions and that we are to be good stewards by protecting and maintaining them. Therefore, our right to self-defense is unalienable. Christians believe that the good news of the gospel of Jesus Christ will destroy the ill news of the Democrats and therefore support the courage of free speech, not the cowardice of censorship. Christians believe that the fear of GOD is the beginning of all knowledge, not that all knowledge lives in Hollywood.

What is it all about? Why do we all toil? Why do Democrats march, riot, loot, and burn? These tragedies are indications of extreme tribulation. What are we all seeking? We are all seeking PEACE. Christians find this peace in Jesus Christ. Too many non-Christian Democrats have no peace. They are, therefore, consumed with drug abuse, LGBTQ, envy, strife, and fears.

Mark 9:42 "Whoever *causes* [author's italics] one of these little ones who believes in me to stumble, it would be better for him if with a heavy millstone hung around his neck and he had been cast into the sea."

I hope the leadership of the Democrat Party can swim.

What is cause? As a noun, "cause" is defined as "a person or thing that gives rise to an action, phenomenon, or condition." As a verb, "cause" is defined as to "make something (especially something bad) happen." Cause introduces another dominant party into an action. This party, once known, is weighted with all responsibility, while the other party or parties are left blameless. In other words, if a man is driving a car and wrecks it, killing two other people, and if it is discovered that some other party "caused" the accident, the man driving the car is found blameless.

Children depend on adults for moral guidance. In the absence of parents, the youth turn to adults with the mantle of authority. These adults are obligated to render moral and legal advice to an inquiring child. Adults also seek professional advice from specialists in certain fields. These fields could include doctors, lawyers, mechanics, and teachers. If it is discovered that willful disinformation or actions are relayed in any of these fields of expertise, the specialist will be found to have caused the damage and will be held responsible for the damages, not the client.

Likewise, Jesus clearly laid out the repercussions for anyone who causes one these young ones to stumble. How would someone cause someone else to stumble? Mostly, by intentionally providing corrupt advice and counsel to the young, causing them to err against the word of GOD.

Accordingly, Democrats consistently advise all Americans, but especially the young, to sin against GOD. They advise and provide aid for them to kill their children, fornicate, indulge in drug use, refrain from religious observance, disobey parents, be slothful or envious, engage in theft, and so on. Per the definition of cause, these young will not be held responsible for these atrocities, but the provocateurs who caused them to sin will carry this punishment. The apostate ministers, abortion doctors, Hollywood pornographers, public school administers, and Democrat politicians better get ready for the millstone and an ocean view.

The concept of cause can assist us in understanding the responsibility and motives behind the Democrats' organized deconstruction of America. The brilliant disguise of commandeering, exploiting, and then debasing the arts is commonly used by evil empires like Iran, North Korea, and Cuba to subdue and control the masses. This technique is now expertly wielded in the United States today by the Democrats. Consider a few of these: The NFL and the NBA are marketing a Marxist, anti-Christian, anti-family organization called Black Lives Matter. Netflix released *Cuties*, a movie considered by many to be a glamorization of pedophilia and child pornography. And in December 2020, *Time* magazine named "WAP" (Wet Ass P#sy) by Cardi B. as the second-best song of 2020. One would have to be blind not see the hand of Satan working in all this.

These people in the Democrat Party leadership who call themselves Christians are identified as liars in 1 John 2:4 (ESV): "Whoever says 'I know him' but does not keep his commandments is a liar, and the truth is not in him." Therefore, evildoers are described as liars who are willful and unrepentant violators of the Ten Commandments. I am here to call the righteous, not the sinners, to repentance. So, let's explore how the Democrat Party compares:

- Which Party violates "Thou Shalt Not Kill" because they want to legalize and finance the murder of millions of innocent children?

- Which Party violates "Thou Shalt Not Steal" because they want to confiscate the property of a wealthy minority population and distribute it to their supporters?

- Which Party violates "Remember the Sabbath Day" because they want to ban religious expression?

- Which Party violates "Thou Shalt Not Take the LORDS Name in Vain" because they want to support Hollywood, hip-hop culture, and the porn industry?

- Which Party violates "Thou Shall Not Make Any Graven Images" because they fight to outlaw the free worshipping of GOD but encourage the worship of dead celebrities and politicians.

- Which Party violates "Honor Thy Father and Mother" because they want to deny parental choice in education and deny parental notification for minor children regarding contraception, abortion, and sex education?

- Which Party violates "Thou Shalt Not Covet" because they want to complain about income inequality, plot wealth redistribution, and then burn and loot their neighbor's possessions while thirsting for revenge and entitlement?

- Which Party violates "Thou Shalt Not Commit Adultery" because they want to advocate for the LGBTQ agenda, women's liberation, and immorality?

- Which Party violates "Thou Shalt Have No Other GODs Before Me" because regarding gender, marriage, affirmation, and obedience, they want to violate the laws of GOD and demand, under severe penalty, that man is to be obeyed?

- Which Party violates "Thou Shalt Not Bear False Witness against Thy Neighbor" because they want to lie to the American people with extreme efficiency and lethality, thus fulfilling their thirst for blood and death while destroying the last great hope for man on this earth—the United States of America?

- To all of the ten aforementioned questions there is only one answer: the Democrats. Ergo: the Democrat Party ideology is evil.

Revelations 21:8 describes the actions of evildoers as the actions of the Democrat Party. They are described as the faithless, murderers, sexually immoral, sorcerers, idolaters, and all liars.

The Democrat Party is not evil because they hate Christianity nor because they have murdered over one hundred million Americans since their inception in 1800 (that would be enough). They are evil because, to achieve this, their leadership lies. Their actions are deliberate. These lies are designed to turn well-meaning Christians into unknowing accomplices of the most unspeakable crimes in history. For centuries, these Democrats have led people of goodwill astray and are stumbling blocks to those seeking salvation. Their actions were foretold. Our Bible speaks of them.

Proverbs 4:14–16 reads: "*Do not set foot on the path of the wicked or walk in the way of evildoers. Avoid it, do not travel on it, pass away from it, pass on. For they cannot rest until they do evil; they are robbed of sleep till they make someone stumble.*"

The great advertising experts know that people want to believe that everything will be okay. For this reason, Obama, shrewdly ran his campaign on "Hope," manipulating a population that had given up on GOD. Since this population has traded GOD for government, their lives have gotten much worse. Because government cannot give the thing that you seek most of all: PEACE. Peace comes from Jesus Christ.

About peace, in John 16:33 Jesus said, "*I have said these things to you, that in me you have peace. In the world you will have tribulation.*"

He said in John 14:27, "*Peace I leave with you; my peace I give to you. Not as the world gives to you. Let not your hearts be troubled, neither let them be afraid.*"

In Philippians 4:7 it is written: "*And the peace of GOD, which surpasses all understanding, will guard your hearts and minds through Christ Jesus.*"

The unification of Black and White Christians is our fight. This task cannot be farmed out to others. It cannot be done by the politicians. This "Great Commission" is the churches' burden. If we do not do it, it will not be done.

Democrats will attempt to kill us all before they allow this.

Everything Jesus commands of us, the Democrats say, "No." Therefore, for Democrat Party ideology to expand, Christianity must be destroyed. Sadly, too many Christians are helping the Democrats. These Christians help the Democrats because Democrats lie.

Christians of all races, colors, genders, and nationalities must leave the Democrat Party. This party is an affront to GOD and the enemy of mankind. If Christians can come together and resist the lies and the instigations from the Democrat Party, we will usher in the Kingdom of Heaven.

CHAPTER 15:

LIE #14—PEDOPHILIA IS NOT A SEXUAL ORIENTATION

DEMOCRATS CONTEND THAT THE Fourteenth Amendment protections should be applied to people's sexual orientation. However, there is a snag: some sexual orientations are more equal than others. Democrats are well aware that some sexual orientations, like pedophilia and necrophilia, are viewed more unfavorably by the American people than others. Just as Democrats denied their intent to legalize homosexuality and transgenderism at the height of its unpopularity in the 1970s but still pushed it through, they have every intention to legalize pedophilia. Democrats have passed their law-granting protections based on sexual orientation, with no exceptions; now they must prepare the ground for these orientations.

In this chapter, I will prove:

1. Democrats believe all sexual orientations should be legal.

2. Pedophilia, along with other unsavory sexual acts, is a sexual orientation that Democrats are working to legalize and protect.

3. Democrats use the politically correct term "sexual orientation" because everyone has one and would like to have it protected. But by doing this they have knowingly obliterated all taboos while being able to deny it.

"But whoso shall cause one of
These little ones who believe in
Me to fall, it was better for him
that a millstone were hung about
his neck, and that he were drowned
in the depth of the sea."

—Matthew 18:6

On April 5, 2021, in an interview on One America News, Tennessee's Republican senator Marsha Blackburn revealed a bit of information that proves my charge that the Democrat Party leadership consists of evil beasts who walk this world with earthly feet.

She described a recent visit she took to the southern border in her capacity as a US senator with some of her colleagues. During this visit, she learned from the US Border Patrol and social workers that 25 percent of all the children detained were there with adults who could not prove that these children belonged to them. These children numbered in the thousands. Many of these children, she said, were, in fact, abducted and brought to America to engage in the illegal and illicit pedophile sex trade industry. To put an end to this exploitation, Senator Blackburn said that she brought to the floor of the Senate a bill titled the END Child Exploitation Act. It would require that in such circumstances, the Border Patrol would be required to conduct a DNA test proving the parentage of the child. This DNA test would only take ninety minutes. According to Senator Blackburn, the Democrats blocked the bill.

Why would they do that? Just keep reading.

In the summer of 2020, Netflix debuted the movie *Cuties*, the series *AJ and the Queen*, and the third season of the Netflix series *Ozark*. *Cuties* is a movie that sexualizes preteen girls. *AJ and The Queen* glamorizes the relationship between a preteen boy and a male drag queen. And *Ozark* glamorizes a sexual relationship between a teenaged boy and a woman old enough to be his grandmother. This is just a small example of how the Democrat Party and their partners in Hollywood are preparing America for their pedophilia offensive. I don't watch a lot of Hollywood TV, so these three television shows are all I know of. But I am sure there are many more.

WebMD defines a pedophile as a person who has a sustained "sexual orientation" toward children generally aged thirteen or younger. Dr. James Cantor of the Centre for Addiction and Mental Health (CAMH) says pedophilia is a "sexual orientation." A sexual orientation is defined by to whom you are attracted and with whom you want to have sex. And according to Democrats, you should have federal protection for that. No exceptions. Democrats know this, but they say pedophilia is exempt because Democrats know most Americans frown on this particular sexual orientation. Today the truth would destroy them. So, like the 1970s and '80s regarding homosexuality, gay marriage, and transgenderism, Democrats play for time. *And lie!* While taking NAMBLA (North America Men/Boy Love Association) money and putting liberal judges on the courts who will do their dirty work for them, they labor to infiltrate more Democrats into government positions. They will bide their time. And they will lie until they are ready to spring their trap: legalization of pedophilia.

Don't doubt me. I have never heard the word "except" in their mantra: "You can't help who you love," "Marry whom you love," and "The heart wants what the heart wants" are what Democrats advertise. Furthermore, all of you who accept this mantra are accomplices to this Democrat pedophile ring.

According to a September 18, 2015, article in *Psychology Today*, before 1973 homosexuality was listed as a classification of mental disorders in the *Diagnostic and Statistical Manual of Mental Disorders* (*DSM*). In 1973, the American Psychiatric Association (APA) voted 5,845 to 3,810 to remove it from the *DSM*. This removal was the beginning of the LGBTQ takeover of the Democrat Party.

According to a November 1, 2013, Huffington Post article, the same American Psychiatric Association that removed homosexuality from the *DSM* is now preparing the ground to remove pedophilia. It says:

> In a move toward destigmatizing pedophilia, the American Psychiatric Association (APA) in its updated *Diagnostic and Statistical Manual of Mental Disorders* (*DSM*), distinguishes between pedophiles who desire sex with children, and those who act on those desires.... The change in the *DSM*, a kind of Bible among medical professionals, lawmakers, and drug and insurance companies, doesn't just apply to pedophilia, but to several other deviant sexual desires listed in the manual. It represents "a subtle but crucial difference that makes it possible for an individual to engage in consensual atypical sexual behavior without inappropriately being labeled with a mental disorder," explains the APA in its DSM-5 Paraphilic Disorders Fact Sheet."

This is just another step toward the perverted aims of the DNC. NAMBLA is an organization of proud pedophiles and is a proud subset of the Democrat Party. They would like to rescind all laws that enforce the age of sexual consent. They believe that children should legally be allowed to have sex at any age without the permission of anyone. On September 22, 2011, Andrew Gumbel wrote a piece for the UK edition of *The Independent* called "Republicans say top Democrats support 'group of gay pedophiles.'" Gumbel states, "Ms. [Nancy] Pelosi had been on gay pride parades where NAMBLA members were also present and had thus been 'marching with pedophiles.'"

ABC News reported on August 31, 2000, "The American Civil Liberties Union is defending a group that supports pedophilia against a civil suit filed by the family for a molested and slain Massachusetts boy." The American Civil Liberties Union (ACLU) is the legal arm of the Democrat Party.

You did not hear about the Democrat Party blocking Senator Blackburn's END Child Exploitation Act because the liberal media covered it up. Pedophiles do exist. Some of them are very rich and very powerful, and donate large amounts of money to Democrat Party politicians. Democrat financier Jeffrey Epstein is probably one of the richest and best known of the group. They need fresh bodies, and the southern border provides them.

Democrats know pedophilia is a sexual orientation. They are building the foundation to make it a reality with the help of many unknowing participants in the Christian community, especially the Black church.

I know. You don't believe me. You say, "No one is that evil and corrupt." Remember, the Devil's greatest trick was convincing mankind that he no longer existed. Go online. Check out everything I just wrote. When you discover that it is true, what are you going to do about it?

CHAPTER 16:

LIE #15—BLACK DEMOCRAT LEADERS CARE ABOUT BLACK PEOPLE

IT IS AMAZING! For Black Americans, everyone instinctively knows that the last sixty years have been a failure. The 2020 riots and protests verify this. But, like a lost man turning around and making the wrong turn over and over again in the same exact spot, the Black community does this when they decide to follow the same compromised Black Democrat Party leadership time and time again.

There is a cultural genocide occurring in real time here in America. It is happening to Black Americans and is carried out by the Democrats. Black Democrats are collaborators. They care nothing for the Black community. Isn't it obvious?

In this chapter, I will prove:

1. The condition of the Black American community is by design. It is, in fact, a cultural genocide.

2. Black leaders are paid contractors hired by liberals to give credibility to this cultural genocide.

3. Republican evacuation of the Black community made this genocide easier.

4. As long as the majority of Black people follow the Democrat Party, they will remain at the bottom in America.

"It was you, Charley."

—Terry Malloy (Marlon Brando) from the movie *On the Waterfront*

"Like children, [Negroes] require government in everything…or they will run into excesses."

—Samuel A. Cartwright, 1851

"Youse a nigga Toby, plain old nigga is all. And what you think you is don't matter a damn bit." In the movie *Roots*, this was the response given by the "house Negro" Fiddler in response to the "field Negro" Toby sharing his proud African heritage of chieftains. Sadly, Black Americans receive the same response from house Negro politicians when Black Americans speak of school choice, the right to keep and bear arms, religious liberties, overpolicing, and economic empowerment. They are reminded that they are not only seen as "niggers" by White Democrats but by the Black Democrat leadership as well. This response isn't given in words like in the past. No, this response is illustrated in the only place where it really counts. It is illustrated in deeds. The deeds prove beyond a shadow of a doubt that Black Democrat politicians hold their constituents in utter contempt!

Black Democrats fought viciously against the Conservative Republican welfare reform acts of the 1990s. However, a March 9, 2021, op-ed in the *Washington Post* titled "Goodbye, Clinton welfare reform. Hello, child tax credit", Charles Lane spoke about how through employing former welfare recipients, the program had been quite successful at alleviating poverty in the Black community. The piece continued and explained how Democrats were scheming to pay these citizens just as much money not to work at all, thus addicting them to sloth and government dependency. The piece reads:

> It has been nearly 25 years since President Bill Clinton's signature domestic policy achievement: the 1996 welfare reform bill based on the idea that poor people must work or seek work, in return for cash benefits.
>
> His fellow Democrats are marking the occasion by abandoning that premise of the Clinton reform, albeit by implication. An expansion of a separate child tax credit in the new pandemic relief package will grant even families with no income or tax liability up to $3,000 per child, ages 6 to 17, and $3,600 for children under 6 this year. They'll get cash, payable in periodic installments, whether anyone in the household works or not....
>
> For a country long committed to the concept that "able-bodied adults" should support themselves, and that any other approach risks discouraging people to participate in the labor force, the governing party's push for no-

> strings-attached family income support reflects major ideological change....
>
> By 2019, child poverty had fallen to 14.4 percent, almost the 1969 low, and welfare rolls had shrunk to just 2 million people, less than a fifth of what they had been in Clinton's time.
>
> For Black children, the poverty drop was especially striking, from 46.6 percent in 1992 to 26 percent in 2019, though the latter figure remains roughly triple that for Whites.
>
> Teen pregnancy, labeled by Clinton "our most serious social problem" in his 1995 State of the Union address, fell from 62 births per 1,000 in 1991 to 17.4 in 2018.
>
> Violent crime, linked to multigenerational welfare dependency in many 1990s analyses, has also fallen dramatically in the past quarter-century, despite a recent uptick....

Government dependency and enticing another generation of Black Americans to choose the plantation is the intention of these Democrat policies. Fearing the responsibilities of freedom, integration-minded Negro Democrat collaborators are verifying every racist stereotype regarding the inability of Black people to exercise freedom by seeking to re-enslave Black people to their masters' Democrat Party. Like a pet dog scratching on his master's door after a bathroom break, these Negro collaborators' hearts ache to be near their owner.

The integration-minded Negros in the Civil Rights Movement gave White Democrats permission to conduct a cultural genocide against Black people in the United States of America. The Black elite so loved the White Democrat and hated Black culture that their primary concept of success was to become like his master. Consequently, the Black elite of America decided to do something never even considered in world history. They protested, boycotted, and died in an effort to surrender the culture of their people and begged to replace it with the culture of their former masters. The master, however, did not want them. No federal government program or law would change their minds. To quote Alabama Governor George Wallace in 1963:

> In the name of the greatest people that ever trod this earth, I draw the line in the dust and toss the gauntlet before the feet of tyranny, and I say: "segregation now, segregation tomorrow, segregation forever."

After hearing this racist statement from the White Democrat governor of Alabama, Black leaders advised Black Americans to become stalkers of racist Democrat White America, instead of Black leaders advising Black Americans to avoid this racist like the plague. And to this day they still beg for the love of a master who hates them. The Black Caucus, NAACP, and Black Lives Matter keep stalking White Americans like scorned lovers. Serving up poor and middle-class Blacks is the price Black leaders are willing to pay to sit at their master's table.

DEMOCRAT LEADERSHIP HATES WALMART

One example of the hatred Democrats have for Black America is the insane hatred the Democrat Party has for Walmart. Walmart has provided, for poor Blacks and Whites, fresh vegetables, fresh food, pharmacies, clothing, and numerous other items that were completely unattainable for African Americans and the poor. Walmart provided jobs and has raised the standard of living all over America. Every person I know rich or poor, but especially every poor Black person, depends on Walmart and loves Walmart. My family and I love Walmart. Nevertheless, on June 6, 2016, *Fortune* magazine reported:

> *Conservatives* showed a preference for Walmart. Liberals put Walmart as the No. 1 company on the Fortune 500 that is the worst for America. They also ranked it as first on a list of companies in the *Fortune* 500 they would like to shut down....

As a child, when Walmart came to Brownsville, Tennessee, our family and community standards of living increased sevenfold. Items that were out of our grasp and impossible to attain became accessible. The racism of the old mom-and-pop stores and their substandard inventory was a distant terrible memory because Walmart did not discriminate and provided excellent customer service; this why Democrats hate Walmart.

Absolute power is the goal of the Democrat Party leadership. This power can only be attained if the Democrat Party controls 90 percent of the Black vote. Democrats will continue to control this vote only by keeping Black Americans poor, unhealthy, and afraid. Walmart is a danger to that plan and must be minimized.

On July 12, 2018, *Newsweek* reported that on August 26, 2016, in a text to former FBI lawyer Lisa Page, fired FBI agent and Democrat operative Peter Strzok wrote, "Just went to a Southern Virginia Walmart. I could smell the Trump support." Rep. Bob Goodlatte read aloud in the hearing "and smell is in capital letters."

If Democrat leadership loves Black people as they claim, how could they hate what we love? And Black people love Walmart.

I shower every day. If they want to call me a "smelly Walmart shopper," I'll carry the moniker proudly.

IF SLAVERY IS A CHOICE NOW, IT WAS CHOICE THEN

Even though most Black Democrats cannot comprehend it, as with all things, slavery is a choice. Of all the terrible plagues of slavery, the curse that convinces the slave that he is powerless and cannot change his circumstances is the worst. The Democrat masters have so poisoned the mind of Black Americans that to consider that we had some part to play in our fate is akin to blasphemy. Because Democrats know if Black people ever realize that their ancestors had a role in their own slavery and could have controlled their circumstances, then Black people today will understand that they can control and therefore change their individual circumstances. They will tear off the yoke of the Democrat oppressor, thus controlling their own destiny.

Democrats fear that Blacks may find this truth and understand that the foundation on which all America stands rests not on the slave but on the descendants of slaves. More than that, they fear if the Conservative movement, like the abolitionist movement and the Union Army, ever unleash the power of the Black Christian Conservative, then the Democrats are finished. Black Conservatives have always been the secret weapon. And we've always defeated the Democrats. But in fighting this evil, we must never forget to love those who hate us.

Because the Civil Rights Movement was a political movement described as a Christian one, it did very little to bring Black and White people together. Coercion is never a good incentive.

Let's admit it, the inner cities were devoid of White people in the 1960s, and they are devoid of White people now. White people and Black people are still segregated, living apart from each other. White culture flourishes. Black culture is dying.

When a people are forced to give up their ethnicity, they are, in fact, dead. Through integration, Democrats are destroying the things that make Black Americans Black. They are destroying Black schools, Black businesses, Black colleges, the Black family, Black church, and the Black middle class.

Blacks started to complain that the lack of Black role models was the problem. So, Black Democrats decided to provide us with role models. Who did they provide? They provided hip-hop artists, Hollywood pornographers, criminals, tattooed athletes, sellout politicians, and apostate preachers. All of them victims. All of them elitists advising young Black people that because of racism they do not have the ability to become as successful in America as these Black elitists have.

What was the inevitable result of a victimization message that says, "You are not free, and you are treated unfairly, oppressed, discriminated against, and held down on account of your race"? Hatred, violence, envy, burning cities, and death.

Black collaborators gave the Black community back to their White Democrat masters on a silver platter. The inner city is a dystopia. The prison is the university, and most young Black men and women are unrecognizable from their ancestors in actions and appearances. Black people may not have integrated with White Democrats socially, but they have integrated politically. Collaborating Black leaders have convinced most Black people to accept the tenets of the evilest party in history.

To paraphrase former British Prime Minister Margaret Thatcher, "European nations are a product of history, America is a product of philosophy." The American philosophy dictates that you cannot trust government and you cannot trust politicians. History has proven this to be true. Most Black Americans, Democrats, and Nazis do not believe this and therefore have decided to hold politicians as godlike figures. And they have suffered for it.

Philosophy had warned the founders, all learned men, not to trust government. History had borne out the fact that government was at best a necessary evil, to be tolerated, moderated, and controlled. The founders trusted each other, if they were friends, but never did they trust each other while governing. When given the opportunity to create a government from scratch, they verified this fact by producing a flawed government that empowered only White men and crushed everyone else. They, therefore, wrote a constitution that listed many things that government could not do. In order to live this way, they understood that they could not fear living as free men and trusted that others would.

This fear of freedom takes us to the fundamental problem of Democrats and Nazis. Democrats and Nazis care nothing about their fellow countrymen. Wherever these two parties maintain power, filth, crime, poverty, and privation are forced upon the good people who live there. Ironically, the worse an area becomes, the higher the politicians who represent that area move up in the Democrat Party. This sinister system is a facsimile of the old slave system where the house Negro was given status and rewards by his master based upon how well he kept the field slaves in line. The occupation of these Black Democrat collaborators still exists. Their titles have changed. They are now called congressman, mayor, delegate, and sometimes senator or president.

We will examine one of these Black Democrat collaborators: Congressman Jim Clyburn from South Carolina and his Sixth Congressional District.

The Wikipedia page of the South Carolina's Sixth Congressional District verifies the before-mentioned story of "Operation Ratf*%K" when the Republican National Committee's Lee Atwater and Ben Ginsberg collaborated with the Black Caucuses to create majority-Black districts in an effort to turn the other districts lily-white and potentially more Republican. It reads: "*The district's current configuration dates from a deal struck in the early 1990s between state Republicans and Democrats in the South Carolina General Assembly to create a majority-black district.*"

From my personal experience in South Carolina politics, I know that since this deal gave the congressional delegation and General Assembly over to the Republican Party for the first time in over one-hundred years. White Democrats were cut out of this deal and are still livid. Republicans and Black Democrats had what they wanted. White Democrats were left powerless. I am sure Republican evacuation, along with withdrawal of all financial support for future candidates, was a vital element of this deal in the Sixth District and every majority-Black district created. From personal experience, I know that the Republican National Committee hasn't seriously funded any Republican candidate, regardless of race or gender, in this district or any majority-Black district since their creation in 1994. Consequently, the Black community, for almost thirty years, has been trapped in a one-party communist system, complete with dictator worship and forced compliance. Because of the Republican National Committee's abandonment of the Black community, I will always consider myself a conservative, but until they correct this injustice, I can no longer consider myself a Republican.

The Republican Party again has relegated themselves to spectators, witnessing the Democrat Party's annihilation of the Black community. As Holocaust survivor Elie Wiesel said, "The opposite of love is not hate, it's indifference." Concerning the Black community, Republican Party leadership is precariously close to indifference.

This corrupt bargain favored the politicians only. This was the Middle Passage in reverse. Previously, Whites bought Black African slaves from other Black Africans. In 1989, Whites sold the Blacks to Black Democrats. This should not be surprising. In his book *Rules for Radicals* Saul Alinsky said: "Political realists see the world as it is: an arena of power politics moved primarily by perceived immediate self-interests, where morality is rhetorical rationale for expedient action and self-interest." Black Americans still make the fatal mistake of believing that Black politicians are the only politicians who are not immoral.

The common denominator here is the sad fact that most Black Americans are still content to be sold like cattle. They are content to be used as pawns, and now even their Black leaders, like Jim Clyburn, hold them in absolute contempt.

Consider this: The Center for American Progress reported in 2020 that out of the 435 congressional districts in the United States, Jim Clyburn's Sixth District ranked 428 in overall poverty; only seven other districts were poorer. Poverty among children was worse, where the Sixth District ranked 433 out of 435. More illuminating, since 2014, when this information was first gathered, South Carolina's Sixth District was ranked 419. Rep. Jim Clyburn's district has fallen nine spots in six years. With this track record you'd think Clyburn would lose all credibility. Ironically, since 2014, Clyburn has been promoted by the Democrats and is now the most powerful Black politician in America. Ergo, for Black people to merit promotion in the Democrat Party, the continual privation of the people in these majority-Black districts is the key to leadership.

Nevertheless, because most Black Americans refuse to exercise due diligence as citizens, remove this incompetent from office, and allow political competition, the collaborator Jim Clyburn is allowed to subjugate this area of Black America in the name of his masters and benefactors in the Democrat Party.

The evidence provided proves that Clyburn has not been re-elected for the past twenty-six years because he is a good congressman. He is in fact, in every metric, an absolute failure. Like a fat drunk defeating an opponent without any arms and legs, Jim Clyburn, like every Black Democrat, is winning elections by default. They don't even raise money in their districts. The vast majority of their money comes from out-of-state White liberals. Black Democrats press the White liberal agenda while maintaining their roles as poverty pimps in the Black community.

After so much death, poverty, and despair, if Clyburn or any of these Black Democrats cared at all for their people, they would not only resign, they would also apologize for ever asking to be elected. Furthermore, if not intended, they would repent for all the damage they and their party have inflicted on Black America.

Sadly, Republican leadership is so risk adverse, they will never invest the capital necessary to flip a majority-Black district. Democrats, however, funneled hundreds of millions of dollars into red state Georgia, allowing a broke thirty-three-year-old documentary film maker (Jon Ossoff) and an apostate Black preacher (Raphael Warnock) all the ammunition they needed to defeat two sitting millionaire US senators and flip the US Senate, thus giving Democrats absolute control over the United States government.

Republican leadership has never shown such resolve, and as of this writing, I am sure they are collaborating with the various state Black Caucuses in an effort to not earn but gerrymander their way into power.

For Black people and Christians, the Democrat Party is a party of death. They do not believe in truth. The Black community exists within the Fourth Reich. To either kill them all or make them totally unrecognizable from their former selves is the Democrat Party end game for Black Americans. They have killed millions through abortion, drugs, murder, and imprisonment. And they have transformed millions through reeducation, mental castration, and religious separation. The Democrat Party leaders are beasts that walk this earth with human feet. Flee them! Become an independent following the word of GOD and voting only for those who will do the same.

In the Book of Deuteronomy chapter 30, GOD said, "I lay before you blessings and curses, life and death; Choose life so that you and thy children will live." The Black community chose the curse of the Democrat Party. Consequentially, over sixty million children were aborted and did not live because of this evil choice.

The lesson: Black Democrats are politicians; not only are they not better than any other politicians—they are worse. Much worse. Even though most White politicians are not any good, they at least have no problem with their districts excelling and doing better. Sadly, the destitution and privation of majority-Black districts are a prerequisite for the promotion of a Black Democrat. And they are prolific at achieving this end.

Black Democrat politicians are supervising the cultural genocide of their own people. They are not heroes. They are not saviors. They are not saints. They are not trustees. They are politicians. Never to be trusted, to always bear suspicion. Double that with Jim Clyburn. To them, you are nothing more than a vote. You are "cannon fodder." To them, you are a human being who deserves to be impoverished and controlled.

Here is the good news. They can only continue this cultural genocide with your permission. Stop giving it! They are looking out for their best interest. Isn't it time that you looked out for yours?

CHAPTER 17:

LIE #16—LIFE DOES NOT BEGIN AT CONCEPTION

THIS CHAPTER WILL BE SHORT. Does life begin at conception? If it does, is abortion murder? The Democrat Party and the Nazis seem not to care. In this chapter, I will prove three things:

1. Life does begin at conception.

2. Democrats know life begins at conception, but they must lie because if you knew the truth, you would destroy them.

3. Democrats promote "abortion pride" because they know repentance will lead to forgiveness. And forgiveness will lead to reconciliation with GOD. Pride will not allow repentance. Democrat leadership will not allow reconciliation.

"The thief comes to kill, steal, and destroy."

—John 10:10

According to theologian Gary Manning Jr. from Biola University, in the Bible verse above the thief is not Satan as many have believed. Manning says:

> So the overall context, moving from John 9–10, down to the discourse, and then down to the parable in John 10:7-10, makes it clear that the thief is a reference to the failed leaders of Israel.... The commenters of the Reformation era up through the nineteenth century all agreed that the thief referred to failed human leaders and their false teaching.

Which leaders preach theft through overtaxation? The Democrats. Which leaders promote the destruction of family, religion, traditions, gender, and all that is good? The Democrats. Which leaders preach death through abortion, euthanasia, drug legalization, disarmament, and poverty? The Democrats.

The thief must kill; it is his nature. They get pleasure from it. They lie about it because they know it is evil. There is no explaining it. There is no rhyme or reason to it. Like a cancer or a hurricane, it is their nature. You cannot change it.

Life is defined as the condition that distinguishes animals and plants from inorganic matter, including the capacity for growth, metabolism, reaction to stimuli, and reproduction. Every person is gifted with each one of these capacities at the time of conception. This is an absolute fact. Democrat Party leadership is drawn to death. Therefore, they must attack life. Democrat Party leadership is cowards. So, they must also attack the weak. Democrat leadership is evil. So, they must attack the innocent.

Our Bible says the thief comes to kill. Theologians agree that the thief is failed human leadership. Democrat leaders are many things, but they are not stupid. Consider the constituents of Democrats and Conservatives. Where are the ghettos, drug dens, failed schools, food deserts, decay, crime, and blight? They are all in Democrat-controlled areas. Despite all the efforts to convince them otherwise, the people living in these inner city areas know that abortion is murder. In these areas, I've been told, the action of aborting a child is described as "putting out a hit." And they call the abortion doctor "the hitman." Chaos is ever present in Democrat-controlled areas. Where chaos reigns, you find a duo that rules as an epoxy: the Devil and the Democrats.

Any sane person understands late-term abortion is murder. However, Democrats have such a callousness for human life, increasing the body count is all that matters. On May 15, 2013, abortion doctor Kermit Gosnell was sentenced to three life terms in prison for, among other things, murdering seven infants born alive. But Democrats would like to make sure no abortion doctor ever goes to prison again for murdering born-alive children. Indeed, on January 30, 2019, AP News reported that Ralph Northam, the Democrat governor of the great state of Virginia and a pediatrician and supporter of late-term abortions, described a hypothetical situation in a radio interview where an infant born alive could be left to die. On February 1, 2019, Anna North for Vox reported it this way: "After appearing to discuss what would happen if a child was born after a failed attempt at abortion, he said, 'the infant would be resuscitated if that's what the mother and family desired, and then a discussion would ensue between the physicians and the mother.'"

Life begins at conception. It ends when growth, metabolism, reaction to stimuli, and reproduction are terminated by laws conceived, maintained, and protected by the lies of the Democrat Party.

CHAPTER 18:

LIE #17—*BROWN V. BOARD OF EDUCATION* HELPED BLACKS

WHAT WAS THE PURPOSE of *Brown v. Board of Education*? Has public education in general and for Black people in particular gotten better? Why do Black people still celebrate Brown? Is forced integration a thing of value? In this chapter, I will prove four things:

1. *Brown v. Board of Education* hurt public education for Black and White students.

2. *Brown v. Board of Education* hurt America.

3. The government educating its citizens is insanity.

4. The primary goal of *Brown* was to turn public education over to the evil Democrat Party and their teachers' unions.

This is the defining excerpt from *Brown v. Board of Education: "Segregation of white and colored children in public schools has a detrimental effect upon colored children…for the policy of separating the races is usually interpreted as denoting the inferiority of the negro group."* How does it help to tell a Black child that he or she is inferior to a White child? Why would people celebrate a Supreme Court decision that stamped them with the badge of inferiority and then told them that the only way to cure their inferiority is to force the people who hate you the most to accept your presence or go to jail? That's precisely what the Supreme Court ruled in *Brown v. Board of Education.* And Black Democrats celebrate this blasphemy while most of America follows its lead.

There is a terrible lie floating through the history of America. This lie has to do with the condition of Southern Black schools before *Brown v. Board of Education.* The lie says that these schools were dirty, unkempt, and ragged shacks, while White schools were clean, well-stocked, and immaculate. Black teachers were illiterate and untrained. White teachers were scholars. Black children were getting a terrible education. White children were brilliant. And every Black parent wanted their child out of their Black school. The converse is actually true.

In the *Brown v. Board of Education*'s written opinion, it states:

> Here, unlike *Sweatt v. Painter*, there are findings below that the Negro and white schools have been equalized, or are being equalized, with respect to buildings, curricula, qualifications and salaries of teachers, and other "tangible" factors.

My mother in-law, Mrs. Chorsie Calhoun, is a retired librarian. Her mother, Mrs. Eaddie Broadwater, was a retired grammar school principal. Both worked in the South Carolina Negro school system. In the family archive exists a wealth of information disproving the lies of the past. The yearbooks and pictures reveal a completely different world than the world depicted by history.

Pictures do not lie. The buildings were not shacks. The children were not dirty, and the teachers were well dressed. The sports teams looked well equipped and ready to play. The men were in suits and the women in dresses. As a matter of fact, the students and teachers of the segregated schools of yesterday look better than the teachers and students in the integrated schools of today.

Black people viewing integration with White America at any cost has been a thing of value to Black Americans since the first Black slave believed that life was better because White people were White and the lives of the Black people were bad because they were Black. Slaves also surmised that Blacks who were closer to Whites also lived better lives. History would like for you to believe that most Black Americans became stalkers. That is a lie!

While other minority groups were demanding institutions of learning that they could control, away from the racist White Americans who hated them, history tells us that Black Americans wanted their children taught by members of the Ku Klux Klan. That is a lie!

I have personal experience with this time in American history. My three older siblings had attended all-Black segregated schools established by and physically connected to churches and loved them. I wouldn't get an opportunity to enjoy the experience. In June 1968, I was five years old. I was about to participate in the Head Start program financed by the federal government and, therefore, would be in the first racially integrated class in the history of Haywood County, Tennessee.

I wanted to ride the bus on that first day. But my father, Ivory Ellison, escorted me to school and stayed with me all day. As he took me home that afternoon, I asked him why he stayed with me at school all day. He said, "Because White men threatened to come to the school and kill all of you, and I stayed there to protect you." I asked him why he would send me to a school like that. He told me, "I wish I could send you to a colored school, but the White folks have closed them all down. I have no choice."

For the rest of the week, he drove me to school and stayed with me, protecting me from the Democrats who wanted to kill me. The next week, after emotions had simmered down and my father had had some harsh conversations with some Klansmen, I was allowed to ride the bus.

Amazingly, this bus-riding experience taught me more about the differences in the Black and White psyche than any other time in my life.

Our bus driver was a White gentleman named Mr. Abbot Smith. Mr. Smith was not cruel to us in any way. He was a perfect Southern gentleman. But when I entered his bus on that first day, I noticed something odd. This was the first integrated school bus in Haywood County history. And Mr. Smith was not going to let the races mix on his bus. He had an invisible line across the middle of the seating section. He had Black children sitting in one half and White children sitting in the other. This division was not drawn side to side. It was drawn front half to back half. Here lies the interesting part. Mr. Smith made the White children sit in the back and made the Black children sit in the front. Amazingly, the White children and their parents did not care.

I have no doubt if it had been reversed and the Black children had been made to sit in the back of the bus, there would have been marches, protests, and boycotts by Blacks. Whites did not care. White people understood that their worth was determined by themselves, not by where they sat on a bus. And not by how they were perceived by other races.

There were no race riots. No ill words. I made friends both Black and White that remain my friends to this day. The grown-ups in the high school did stupid things so they would not upset the feds. Superlatives went to two Blacks, two Whites. Class officers and homecoming queens were alternated by race.

The affluent White families built a private school in Haywood County. They named it "Tennessee Academy." Ironically, as history has led you to believe, we never felt inferior to these students. We actually thought the school was a bit of a joke. Their sports teams were horrible, and their school was a small 1A school. Our school played in the largest high school division in the state (AAA), and our football and basketball teams were perennially in the state top ten.

From my personal experience, every Black person I've ever known has privately told me that integration did terrible harm to the Black community. Very few will admit to this publicly.

Black South Africa has a similar history to that of Black America. Ironically, the BBC on May 29, 2010, reported that many Black South Africans admit that life for Blacks was better under apartheid. The Huffington Post headline on February 12, 2018, was "Is SA [South Africa] Really Worse Now Than Under Apartheid?" At least they are not afraid to talk about it. Most Black Democrats are so cowed by their White Democrat masters that they won't whisper any discontent even while their children die.

Lastly and maybe most important, today's statistics prove that they were wrong and that they failed at every stated goal. On February 12, 2020, the Economic Policy Institute wrote, "Findings on school segregation and student performance come from the National Center for Education Statistics' National Assessment of Educational Progress (NAEP) and they concluded that Black children are 'still relegated to separate and unequal schools.'"

So, what was *Brown v. Board of Education* all about? After the decision was issued by the federal Supreme Court, the federal government became the enforcement arm of the decision. *Brown v. Board of Education* wrested control of public education away from state and local governments while handing it to the federal government and the Democrat Party through its unions. During this time, the teachers' unions have indoctrinated America's children with the Democrat Party attributes of national hatred, race hatred, secularism, victimization, race envy, and jealousy.

Furthermore, for any of you who had a doubt, the 2020 COVID year made it abundantly clear that the teachers' unions control public education. The union does not work for the parents. The parents work for the union and hold them in utter contempt. This why I support school choice. Choicc is freedom. From now on, we should not call it "school choice." We should call it "*educational freedom.*" Why would anyone vote against freedom? After witnessing the disrespect and indifference directed at parents by the public education system and its union, any parent who votes against any political candidate advocating for school choice should compare themselves to the slave volunteering their child to be sold on the auction block or the slave escorting their child to the overseer's quarters for his pleasure.

CHAPTER 19:

LIE #18—GUNS ARE BAD

THERE ARE ALWAYS SLAVES looking for masters and always masters looking for slaves. This dynamic balances the Democrat Party. Slave-minded people seek subjugation. Free people will kill and die before they allow it. To successfully subjugate a free people, the government must disarm them. But in America, the government must first garner the people's permission, and the Democrat Party is demanding it.

In this chapter, I will prove four things:

1. In order to be free, you must be armed.

2. If you choose to disarm yourself, you've chosen to be a slave.

3. The Democrat Party plan to disarm America is also the plan to enslave America.

4. It is not against the laws of GOD to protect what he has given you: your life, freedom, person, family, property, and so forth.

"A free people ought not only be armed but disciplined."

—George Washington

"To disarm the people is the most effectual way to enslave them."

—George Mason

In describing an evil con man, my dad would say, "That no good joker lies so good he'll talk a dog into biting himself." Democrats lie so well they accomplished the human equivalent: they've talked their members into disarming themselves.

Even though there are thousands of statistics and books written that prove guns make communities safer, I will not quote from them. Democrats will only quote skewed or fake counterarguments. I will just deal with the concepts of history and common sense.

Regarding self-defense John Locke wrote:

> And that all men may be restrained from invading others rights, and from doing hurt to one another, and the law of nature be observed, which willeth the peace and preservation of all mankind, the execution of the law of nature is, in that state, put into every man's hands, whereby everyone has a right to punish the transgressors of that law to such a degree, as may hinder its violation: for the law of nature would, as all other laws that concern men in this world be in vain, if there were no body that in the state of nature had a power to ex-

> ecute that law, and thereby preserve the innocent and restrain offenders. And if anyone in the state of nature may punish another for evil he has done, everyone may do so: for in that state of perfect equality, where naturally there is no superiority or jurisdiction of one over another, what any may do in prosecution of that law, everyone must needs have a right to do.

While witnessing the violence and murder during the liquidation of the Krakow ghetto in the movie *Schindler's List*, my twelve-year-old daughter asked the most fundamental question: "Where are their guns? Why don't they fight back?" I had to explain to her that the Nazis treated the Jews like Democrats treat Black people: They relaxed gun laws for Germans as they do for White Americans. Then, mirroring the Black Codes and inner city gun laws of today, in 1938, the Nazis banned Jewish persons from possessing any dangerous weapons, including firearms. And Nazis yesterday, like Democrats today, are attempting to ban all militias except the ones that they approve by designating them domestic terrorist organizations.

With all the riots and violence in 2020, you would think that every argument against the Second Amendment has been obliterated. To paraphrase Michael Corleone in *The Godfather: Part II*, "If anything in this life is certain, if history has taught us anything, it is that *Jews, women, and Blacks always need to be armed!*" Governments do not protect us. If we are protected, this protection is due to a combination of knowledge, money, and firepower. There is no sane counterargument to this pronouncement.

Instead, the Democrat leadership presses forward with their evil agenda. Their lies are amazing. For your own safety, you need a license, a background check, registration, training, and a lockbox, as well as to pass a written test. In addition, there will be some guns you will not be allowed to own, for your own good.

In Matthew 4:7, Jesus said, "*It is written again, Thou shalt not tempt the Lord thy God.*" This commandment simply means that when you can defend yourself and choose not to do so, it is forbidden to ask GOD for help after intentionally putting yourself in dangerous situations. It is "tempting GOD" to play with rattlesnakes and brag that GOD will protect you. It is "tempting GOD" to disarm yourself in the midst of violent men and a tyrannical government. GOD is not a flunky. You cannot call him to make your bed or mow your lawn. He will demand that you do what you are able to do. He will do what you cannot. History is littered with world leaders who "tempted GOD" and were assassinated after refusing to take the appropriate steps regarding their personal security. History is less concerned about the everyday citizens who are murdered each day because they listen to the lies of the Democrat Party and tempt GOD.

Once you vote to allow background checks, your enemies in government will then decide who passes the background check and how long the process will take. As they place more and more restrictions, you will soon find that it will become more and more difficult for law-abiding citizens to pass these tests. You will find people with speeding tickets, tax liens, late child support payments, bad checks, and any misdemeanor offense have their right to keep and bear arms infringed upon. Moreover, because of the demand for gun registration among Democrats, government officials will know the number, the type, and the location of every gun—of every citizen the government chooses to disarm.

These rights are irrevocable, irreversible, and nontransferable. Instead of trying to weaken the rights of the law-abiding, they should secure these rights and watch the crime rates fall. But Democrats know this. Democrats are evil, not stupid. They need power. In order to have power, they need to keep Black people under control. To control Black people, they need them disarmed.

An unknown person has been quoted as saying, "Gun control is like trying to reduce drunk driving by making it tougher for sober people to own cars."

Another unknown person said, "An armed man is a citizen. A disarmed man is a subject."

I have always been enraged by the fact that my government violates and abridges my right to protect my person, my family, and my property as I see fit.

As a law-abiding citizen, without first gaining the government's permission, I am prohibited from carrying a firearm on my person or in my car. Criminals have no such prohibition. They can carry any weapons they desire. Therefore, courtesy of my government, I am placed at a serious disadvantage. My government has served up its law-abiding citizens as prey to the savages of this nation.

This idea of self-defense isn't strange to the strong men of America. But to the weak it appears to be heresy and most of them reside in the Democrat Party. Placed as the second article in his creation of the Organization of Afro-American Unity (OAAU), Malcolm X wrote:

> Since self-preservation is the first law of nature, we assert the Afro American's right to self-defense.
>
> The Constitution of the United States of America clearly affirms the right of every American citizen to bear arms. And as Americans, we will not give up a single right guaranteed under the Constitution. The history of unpunished violence against our people clearly indicates that we must be prepared to defend ourselves or we will continue to be defenseless people at the mercy of a ruthless and violent racist mob.

We assert that in those areas where the government is either unable or unwilling to protect the lives and property of our people, that our people are within our rights to protect themselves by whatever means necessary....

This is the thing you need to spread the word about among our people wherever you go. Never let them be brainwashed into thinking that whenever they take steps to see that they're in a position to defend themselves that they're being unlawful. The only time you're being unlawful is when you break the law. It's lawful to have something to defend yourself.... Why, what kind of fool do you look like, living in a country that will go to war at the drop of a hat to defend itself, and here you've got to stand up in the face of vicious police dogs and blue-eyed crackers waiting for somebody to tell you what to do to defend yourself!

Those days are over, they're gone, that's yesterday. The time for you and me to allow ourselves to be brutalized nonviolently is passe.... It's hard for anyone intelligent to be nonviolent. Everything in the universe does something when you start playing with his life, except for the American Negro. He lays down and says, "Beat me daddy."

So it says here: "A man with a rifle or club can only be stopped by a person who defends himself with a rifle or a club." That's equality.

It is obvious that government doesn't want to protect you, cannot protect you, and actually doesn't even have to protect you and Malcolm knew it. "Protect and Serve," the slogan for every police department, is a lie.

In *DeShaney v. Winnebago County*, the Supreme Court ruled that government agencies do not have the burden of protecting the public from a public actor. Joshua DeShaney was under state protective custody in Wisconsin. His father, Randy DeShaney, was known to beat his children. The state, after restricting access, finally allowed visitation between the father and his children. In March 1984, Randy DeShaney beat four-year-old Joshua so severely that he fell into a life-threatening coma. Joshua died on November 9, 2015, at age thirty-six. Randy DeShaney was convicted of child abuse and served less than two years in jail. The court opinion held that the due process clause protects against state action only, and Randy DeShaney, who abused his son Joshua, was not a state actor. The Winnebago County Department of Social Services was a state actor and therefore not liable. Ergo, the government is not responsible for your safety. When they do not protect you, you have no recourse.

In 1981, the District of Columbia Court of Appeals ruled in *Warren v. District of Columbia* that police do not owe a specific duty to provide police services to citizens. These were the circumstances of the case:

> In the early morning hours of March 16, 1975, Miriam Douglas, Carolyn Warren, and Joan Taliaferro were raped by Marvin Kent and James Morse. During these rapes, the police were called twice and came to the apartments. The police arrived, showed little interest in investigating the goings-on in the apartment, and left. Thus, for the next fourteen hours,

> the women were raped, beaten, robbed, forced to commit sexual acts upon one another, and made to submit to the sexual demands of Kent and Morse.
>
> Douglas, Warren, and Taliaferro decided to sue the District of Columbia and the Metropolitan Police Department on claims of negligence. In a 4–3 ruling, the District of Columbia Court of Appeals decided that "the duty to provide public services is owed to the public at large, and absent a special relationship between the police and an individual, no specific legal duty exists."

You read correctly. The District of Columbia Court of Appeals ruled that the police have no specific duty to assist any citizen. Not you, not me, not anyone. Our government is not assisting the law-abiding citizens. Our government is assisting the criminal.

Nevertheless, with all the criminal activity in the United States, on August 20, 2020, the *Atlantic* reported that "Democrats in 2020 are embracing gun control in an unprecedented way."

The fact that my government forces me to travel hundreds of miles without the means to defend my person, my loved ones, or my property—while encountering strange people, places, and things; and understanding that there are evil predators that seek my life and the lives of the people I love—is absolute tyranny.

All laws restricting a person's inalienable right to keep and bear arms are unjust laws. To quote St. Thomas Aquinas, "An unjust law is no law at all." To go back to my original theme, Democrat Party leadership is evil.

I have never been arrested or charged with a crime. I pay my taxes. I earn my keep. I provide for my family. Nevertheless, because of what others have done, in a government of "pre-venge" (punishment before you commit the crime), I am not allowed to carry a gun to defend myself without the permission of my number one enemy: my government. And history will show that my government has attempted to harm me and those that who like me for centuries.

This is what the great John Locke wrote about the right to self-defense:

> I should have a right to destroy that which threatens me with destruction: for, by the fundamental law of nature, man being to be preserved...the safety of the innocent is to be preferred: and one may destroy a man who makes war upon him, or has discovered an enmity to his being, for the same reason that he may kill a wolf or a lion; because such men are not under the ties of common law of reason, have no other rule, but that of force and violence, and so may be treated as beasts of prey, those dangerous and noxious creatures, that will be sure to destroy him whenever he falls into their power.

Locke also believed that we were placed in this world to do GOD's will and belonging to him, except for self-preservation, we have no right to take any life, not even our own. And because we are here to do the will of GOD, we are also obligated to preserve our own lives. In his *Second Treatise of Government*, Locke wrote:

> [F]or men being all the workmanship of one omnipotent, and infinitely wise maker; all the servants of one sovereign master, sent into the

> world by his order, and about his business; they are his property, whose workmanship they are, made to last during his, not one another's pleasure.... Everyone, as he is bound to preserve himself and not to quit his station willfully.

Soon after the Civil War, at the beginning of Reconstruction, freed Black men made two fatal mistakes. They decided to remain in close vicinity with their former masters ,and too few decided to fight them.

In a piece called "The Arming and Disarming of Black America" in *Slate* magazine, Nicholas Johnson wrote:

> The spectacle of black soldiers with guns and the authority of uniforms grated hard on defeated Confederates. Almost as soon as the shooting war stopped, the Southern governments moved to reinstitute slavery through a variety of state and local laws, restricting every aspect of freedmen's lives. Gun prohibition was a common theme of these "Black Codes."
>
> These sorts of fears fueled overtly racist gun laws like Mississippi's Act to Regulate the Relation of Master and Apprentice Relative to Freemen, which prohibited blacks from owning firearms, ammunition, dirks, or bowie knives. Alabama prohibited "any freedman, mulatto or free person of color in this state, to own firearms, or carry about this person a pistol or other deadly weapon. An 1865 Florida law similarly prohibited "Negroes mulattos or other persons of color from possessing guns, ammunition

> or blade weapons" without obtaining a license issued by a judge on recommendation of two respectable citizens, presumably white. Violators were punished by public whipping up to "39 stripes."

With the riots of 2020, the harassment of Black Men by police, murder at a thirty-year high, and the history of governments (the Soviet Union, Nazi Germany, North Korea, Cuba, and Venezuela) murdering their citizens by the tens of millions, why would any sensible or sane person voluntarily disarm themselves? Simply, they are either cowards, insane, or just desire to be slaves.

Crime statistics be damned. The sensibilities of neighbors be damned. Fear be damned. The right to defend oneself is a right granted by GOD. An unalienable right is irrevocable, indestructible, and nontransferable. They are mine. Gifted to me by GOD and protected by me and the Constitution of the United States of America.

Without gun control, the Democrats could not sell illegal drugs in the Black community. They couldn't forcibly trap Black families in the ghetto or intimidate Black Americans into voting for them. Police wouldn't be able to intimidate, disrespect, and assault Black men. Gun control is the weapon of a tyrant.

America was never meant to be a "police state." Our Second Amendment states, "A well- regulated Militia, being necessary to the security of a free State, the right of the people to keep and bear Arms, shall not be infringed."

The Founders understood that the number-one provocateur of violence was the government. The government, therefore, could not be trusted with the safety and freedom of the people. Government is the entity usually engaged in abolishing your rights.

The "reimagining police" movement is only possible when we understand that the security of a free state stands with the militia. What is the militia? The militia is defined as "a military force raised from the civilian population." This militia must be regulated and armed. What does regulate mean? Democrats want you to believe that regulated means controlled. That is a lie. Jack Rakove, professor of political science at Stanford, said, "Well-regulated in the 18th century tended to be something like well organized, well-armed, well-disciplined." Simply, "regulated" means "ready to fight."

Would crime statistics, neighbor sensibilities, or the fear of others entreat government to abridge my unalienable rights to freedom of speech, religion, press, trial by jury, or assembly? Then why should these sentiments affect my right to keep and bear arms? Democrats understand that all rights rest upon this one right. If it falls, they all fall. That is their plan.

CHAPTER 20:

LIE #19—CONSERVATIVES ARE THE ENEMY OF BLACK AMERICANS

WHAT IS CONSERVATISM? Democrats have consistently told Blacks that Conservatives were and still are the racists. Therefore, the political ideology of Conservatism must also be racist. Since most conservatives live in the Republican Party, Republicans must also be racists and are the enemy of Black people. In this chapter, I will prove five things:

1. Conservatives are not the enemy of Black people.
2. The racist organizations that exist in America are not conservative, they are, in fact, liberal and Democrat.
3. Conservatism is aligned with the Christian ideology.
4. Most Black Americans are conservative and are exploited and manipulated by Democrat Party lies and fight against their own interests.

5. White Democrats have been successfully convincing Blacks to hate conservative Christian abolitionists for the past 220 years.

"For anything we say or do, the slaves would scarcely know there is a Republican Party. I believe they would not, in fact, generally know it for your misrepresentations of us, in their hearing."

—Abraham Lincoln, Cooper Union Speech, 1860

During the pre-1865 glory years of the Democrat Party in the Antebellum South, the abolitionists were their archenemy. By 1840, more than 15,000 people were members of abolitionist societies. The unconditional abolition of slavery in the United States was the goal of the abolitionist movement. In an effort to convince Black people to continue to participate in their own oppression, Democrats lied to their Black slaves regarding the abolitionist's intent. Regarding the intent of Christian abolitionists, Democrats continue to lie to their Blacks captives to this day.

Contrary to the lies of the Democrat Party, most of the abolitionists were conservative Christians. They were not liberal. Let's remember Abraham Lincoln's definition of conservative:" Is it not adherence to the old and tried, against the new and untried?" Racism was a new idea propagated into Christianity by the 1840s. According to Sampie Terreblanche, in the over 2,000 years of Christianity, "racism" is a relatively new phenomenon, especially in the 1800s. He wrote:

> [I]n the first pattern of Western European empires (1530–1820), the myths about the alleged superiority/inferiority of the West/Rest were mainly religious constructs.

Izak J. J. Spangenberg from the University of South Africa, Pretoria, wrote:

> During the second pattern of the Western European empires (1820–1950), full-blown racist ideas were used to legitimize European domination of other people....
>
> Some scholars opine that it was only in the 1850s that the notion of white racial superiority emerged, while others state that the term "racism" was coined around 1930 to counter the Nazis' conviction that they belong to a "superior race."

Democrat Party Christians, instead of allowing Christianity to mold their politics, they allowed their politics to mold their Christianity. While still remaining one of the more racist organizations in the world today, liberal Democrat Party Christians have expanded their blasphemy to support abortion, LGBTQ, religious restrictions, limitations to self-defense, and free speech. Christianity is a religion of life. The Democrat Party is a party of death. They are incompatible.

The Democrats hated the abolitionists, not because the abolitionists sought to steal the Democrats' slaves, but because the abolitionists wanted to assist the slaves in exercising the slaves' freedom. Like today, Black people exercising their freedom would be great for Black people but would have a detrimental effect on White Democrats and their Black collaborators. White Democrat power can only be achieved by maintaining a Black community that is steeped in an endless cycle of poverty, crime, substance abuse, ignorance, and violence. Because of these maladies, Blacks, not being able to support themselves, will have to blindly vote for Democrats. Additionally, since Black unemployment must necessitate Black dependency, an illegal immigrant force will have to be employed to fill the void of the abandoned labor pool of which Blacks have been locked out.

As previously stated, in his "House Divided" speech, Abraham Lincoln saw through the sinister plans and the evil designs the Democrat Party. Lincoln and the abolitionists understood then as we do now that, like their Nazi children, the goal of the Democrat Party was to enslave everyone, not just minorities. The White male, elite Democrat Party hierarchy wanted to deny constitutional and human rights to poor Whites, women, indigenous people, Catholics, and everyone else they deemed unworthy. Lincoln said:

> A house divided against itself cannot stand. I believe this government cannot endure, permanently half *slave* and half *free.* I do not expect the Union to be *dissolved*—I do not expect the house to *fall*—but I do expect it will cease to be divided. *It will become all one thing or all the other.* [Author's italics]

After the notorious Dred Scott case, conservative anti-slavery Whigs and conservative Christian abolitionists started the Republican Party in 1856 specifically to end slavery and adhere to the Constitution of the United States.

Our fight (the abolitionist's fight) remains today. Nothing has changed. As in 1865, and now, 90 percent of Black Americans remain oppressed while still refusing to leave their masters on the Democrat Party plantation. Whereas 10 percent of Black Americans have broken off the yoke of slavery and, like Fredrick Douglass, Harriet Tubman, and the Massachusetts 54th Regiment, are fighting to free them.

Democrats have had a 220-year head start of lies. It is almost impossible to break through. White Democrats have isolated Black Democrats in either Black congressional or House districts or in Democrat-controlled inner city ghettos. Like the Antebellum South, here Democrats control all information, employment, education, housing, crime, and punishment. With this control in the Antebellum South, Democrats taught Blacks to hate and fear conservative Christian abolitionists. With this same control in 2021, the same Democrats teach Blacks to fear conservatives.

Abolitionists first explained to Blacks that they were, in fact, born free, were not slaves, and had an unalienable right and duty before GOD to exercise that freedom.

For the past fifty years, history has forwarded the lie that the Civil Rights Movement was an offensive against American racism and hatred against Blacks, when it was actually a fight against the evils conducted against Black people by White Democrats in both the North and South.

Check your history. Wherever Martin Luther King Jr. led a protest march against racism, discrimination, poverty, and segregation; whether it be Selma and Birmingham or Chicago and Detroit, Democrats were always in charge of the area being protested. This phenomenon is still ongoing to this day. All the riots in Chicago, Minneapolis, Memphis, Los Angeles, and so on, these racist and violent cities are still controlled by Democrats not conservatives. Even the most diehard Democrat must admit this not a coincidence; this is a plan.

Continuing with Lincoln's Cooper Union address, Lincoln said:

> True, we do, in common with "our fathers who framed the Government under which we live," declare our belief that slavery is wrong; but the slaves do not hear us declare even this. For anything we say or do, the slaves would scarcely know…it but for your misrepresentations of

> us, in their hearing. In your political contests among yourselves, each faction charges the other with sympathy with Black Republicanism; and then, to give point to the charge, defines Black Republicanism to simply be insurrection, blood, and thunder among the slaves.

In *The Lego Batman Movie*, the Joker and Batman are again in hand-to-hand combat. Ready to flee, the Joker gleefully reminds Batman that he, the Joker, is Batman's greatest enemy. The Joker is absolutely devastated when Batman reveals to him that the Joker is not his greatest enemy. Batman reveals that the Joker is hardly an afterthought. The Joker lost his purpose. As a narcissist, the belief that Batman spent every waking hour thinking of him fed his ego.

Like the Joker, most Black Democrats believe that White Conservatives spend every waking moment fixated on them. They believe that White conservatives are obsessed with the destruction of them personally. They refuse to even entertain the truth: that like the Joker to Batman, after work, children, church, spouse, relatives, and so on, Black people are an afterthought to most White conservatives.

Most White conservatives have given up on the Black vote. Most White conservatives do not live in majority-Black districts or in the inner city. White Democrats are obsessed with the Black vote. Like the Democrats needing slavery, they now need the Black vote to survive. And they are masters at getting it.

In his Cooper Union speech, Abraham Lincoln slammed the Democrats for attempting to highjack the banner of Conservatism. Lincoln was having none of it. Addressing the Democrats on this issue, Lincoln said:

> But you say that you are conservative—eminently conservative—while we are revolution-

> ary, destructive, or something of the sort. What is conservatism? Is it not adherence to the old and tired, against the new and untried? We stick to, contend for, the identical old policy on the point in controversy which was adopted by "our fathers who framed the Government under which we live;" while you with one accord reject, and scout, and split upon that old policy, and insist upon submitting something new.... Consider, then, whether your claim of conservatism for yourselves, and your charge or destructiveness against us, are based on the most clear and stable foundations.

To clarify, conservatives fight to maintain the tried and true. Liberalism is a fight for constant change. Before and during the Civil War, Lincoln argued that Republicans were fighting to preserve the Constitution, the intent of the founders, and the law by upholding the Northwest Ordinance of 1787, which prohibited slavery in those territories. By fighting to uphold the law and the intent of the founders, Lincoln reasoned that the Republicans were the conservatives. And because the Democrats were fighting to change the law by force, the Democrats were revolutionaries or liberals.

Based on the reasoning of Abraham Lincoln, because the Civil Rights Movement was demanding that the current law be followed (the right to vote, trial by jury, equal protection), the Civil Rights Movement began as a conservative movement. But after the 1965 Voting Rights Act, the movement revealed it true motives. Civil rights was a Trojan horse. Revolutionaries and liberals, once hidden in the movement, began to emerge and exert control. Hell-bent on exploiting Black pain for their gain, they went to work.

The Civil Rights Movement had given the Devil access to Black America; now the Devil is using his Democrats to destroy them. Through this demonic leadership, Blacks became anti-American activists demanding extraconstitutional and socialist programs, like gun control, religious repression, forced integration, busing, the man-in-house-rule, or better known as the man-out clause in welfare, feminism, LGBTQ, government dependency, open borders, pornography, drug legalization, and government education.

These White racist Democrats who fought for the right to subjugate and kill Black people by fighting to ignore the law or overturn the law were the liberals. Liberals consistently fight to upend the Constitution, while conservatives fight to conserve it.

Democrats possess a condescending view of Black Americans. With their admission that they cannot achieve success in America, Black people verify every negative racist stereotype forced upon them by their Democrat masters since slavery. The entire concept of slavery, the plantation system, and the Jim Crow laws of the South was based upon the logic and rhetoric of the inability and inferiority displayed by the Democrat Party today toward Black Americans. Furthermore, their need for federal intervention to secure their unalienable rights from the descendants of their former masters, in addition to the need for further federal assistance to survive in America, is a damning admission to the belief in their own Black inferiority.

Revolutionary actions attempting to overturn or disobey the law through violence are never conservative. In America, our legal foundation rests in the Constitution. There is constant tension regarding this document. The conservative reading of it usually coincides with interpretations that were rendered and have been practiced for generations. Occasionally, someone will decide that this 232-year-old document actually meant something that no one else ever thought it meant. These people are usually liberals.

After over 180 years of existence, some liberal judges discovered that the Constitution did not protect freedom of religion, life, assembly, the right to bear arms, and familial traditions, among other things. Restricting these freedoms hurt not only Black Americans but all Americans.

How do conservatives hurt Black people? By protecting freedom of religion, freedom of speech, freedom of assembly, freedom of press, the right to keep and bear arms, equal protection under the law, the right to keep most of what you earn, and demanding that you work for your bread and fulfill your potential? If these constitutional rights are enforced, conservatives believe that every man and woman will travel as far as their talents will take them. Each plowing that plot of ground that GOD gave them and choosing to be happy.

CHAPTER 21:

LIE #20—REPARATIONS ARE GOOD

EVERY PRESIDENTIAL ELECTION CYCLE, the thorny debate regarding reparations for slavery raises its head. For some reason, Democrats usually latch on to this idea, displaying it before Black Americans as this shiny object easily accessible if only Blacks vote Democrat. In this chapter, I will prove four things:

1. Reparations are fairy tales, told to overly trusting Black people in an effort to keep them waiting in place for a payoff that will never come.

2. Democrats know they are lying.

3. The call for reparations stems from the multiple sins of manipulation, envy, unforgiveness, and pride.

4. Paid reparations will not reconcile Black and White Americans.

*"Forgiveness cannot be earned
and should not be expected or wanted."*

—Ebenezer Scrooge, Christmas Carol

*"Pride is spiritual cancer; it eats up the
very possibility of love, or contentment,
or even common sense."*

—C. S. Lewis

*"O, beware, my lord, of jealousy! It is the
green-eyed monster, which doth mock the
meat it feeds on."*

—William Shakespeare, Othello

As mentioned before, OurTimePress.com's David Mark Greaves estimates that Black Americans are owed $58,000,000,000,000 ($58 trillion) in reparations from the White citizens of the United States. According to RankRed.com, there is only $37 trillion in the entire world. Therefore, all the money in the world is not enough to satisfy these people. Democrats are literally asking for more than all the money in the world as payment for slavery, to give to people who were never slaves, by people who never owned a single slave. Also, I find it ironic that a racist organization calling itself the Democrat Black Caucus is suing America for being racist. America is the country that freed the slaves from the Democrat Party. Nevertheless, the Democrat Party Black Caucus is suing America for the racism and slavery that its party, the Democrats, inflicted upon their ancestors.

It is abundantly clear that the people who advocate such nonsense are insane. But the fact that many of these maniacs walk the halls of Congress is either concerning or terrifying.

If White Americans provide reparations to Black Americas for slavery, why would they be doing it? Are they seeking to buy forgiveness? Are they actually attempting to pay one person for the life work of thousands of previously enslaved descendants? Do they think that this payoff will wash away the original sin of their ancestors? If they genuinely believe any or all of these questions, they are sadly mistaken.

If Black people accept the reparations offered to them by White Americans, will that clear the ledger of all American debts incurred during slavery and Jim Crow? Of course not! To quote the Rev. Dr. Martin Luther King Jr., "We will not be satisfied until justice rolls down like water and righteousness like a mighty stream." That's just a fancy way of saying, "All we know how to do is protest."

So, what is this talk of reparations really about? If it were all about money or compensation for past wrongs, Black Americans would have a stronger claim against the Democrat Party and the African nations than the United States.

Before 1865, all the slaves were concentrated in that part of America controlled by the Democrat Party. After the Civil War, the criminal Jim Crow laws were implemented by that very same party. Today, the inner cities and majority-Black districts where Blacks are isolated, overpoliced, miseducated, murdered, incarcerated, and generally oppressed are still controlled by Democrats.

The northern part of the country and the Republican Party were dedicated to a constant 200-year fight to change these laws and subdue the racism that still exists in Democrat Party.

The African nations were just as guilty. According to a July 19, 2020, story on the BBC, "1.5 million Igbo slaves were shipped across the Atlantic Ocean between the 15th and 19th centuries…through the Calabar port, in the Bight of Bonny." The *Wall Street Journal* reported that historian David Eltis at Emory University showed that "the majority of captives brought to the U.S. came from Senegal, Gambia, Congo, and eastern Nigeria." According to PBS, between 1525 and 1866, 12.5 million slaves were shipped to the New World. About 388,000 were shipped to North America, although Professor Robert Davis of Ohio State University says it was between 1 and 1.25 million.

African Nations have never contributed a dime of restitution for their crimes against Black Americans. They sold us and never sent one canoe to try to reclaim or even check on our welfare. For the past 160 years, the United States government has paid restitution consisting of over 600,000 lives and billions of dollars in property damage in the Civil War, thousands of pages of legislation, and trillions of dollars in social programs.

If Black leaders are serious about demanding payment from the buyers of slaves, they must also demand compensation from the sellers. With the capability of DNA, we can even pinpoint which country sold us. Furthermore, with the power of the US government, we could demand payment from these nations, and they'd have no choice but to comply.

However, Black Democrats never demanded that the two entities most responsible for the slave trade and slavery (African nations and the Democrat Party) pay a dime of reparations. Instead, they insist that the nation that ended it (the United States) pay.

Some could say that Black Americans refused compensation for slavery at the end of the Civil War. According to Dr. Phillip Magness, on August 14, 1862, Lincoln met with a Black delegation at the White House and made a case for colonization. The Black leaders refused. Later in 1863 Lincoln mentioned moving the "whole colored race of the slave states into Texas." Black leaders still disagreed. And when Black and White Republicans controlled the former slave states, they did not fight for reparations.

Instead, many Blacks were too busy working with their former masters in a scheme to return White racist Democrats to power.

So, what is this call for reparations really about? It is manipulation and control. It is shrewd, evil White Democrats casting their sins on the rest of America and convincing ignorant, envious, and prideful Black Democrats that if they grant Democrats their vote, Democrats will force America to pay. This is a lie. To White Democrats, it is all about acquiring the Black vote the way they've always obtained it: through fraud, lies, intimidation, and manipulation. But to Black Democrats, it is all about hatred, envy, and pride. Black Democrats are so blinded by pride, hatred, and envy that they cannot reason. This pride is very destructive. The misleading concept of Black pride has caused many Black Democrats to constantly compare themselves with White America. Comparing oneself to another person is terrible, but comparing one race to another race is insanity. It is a bottomless pit that is forbidden and causes enmity against mankind.

Pride caused the plantation master to treat Black people as slaves. Pride caused the South to refuse all talks of peace and force Civil War. Pride caused White Democrats to create a satanic Jim Crow government bestowing on them absolute power. Pride is causing Black people to not make peace with their nation or even call themselves American.

The sin of pride entices Black athletes to kneel for our national anthem. Pride causes riots, looting, and burning. Pride calls for reparations, quotas, and affirmative action. The sin of pride calls for federal interventions to force Whites to go to school with you, feed you, use the bathroom beside you, or bake a cake for you. In Proverbs 16:18, it is recorded that "pride goeth before the destruction." This is so true, for history has recorded that all these prideful attitudes have led to nothing but misery and strife for most Black Democrats. And the Democrat Party has been the instigator of it all.

The opposite of pride is humbleness. Jesus was humble. If someone refuses to feed you in their restaurant, the humble person will leave, open a better restaurant, and feed the person who would not feed him. If someone refuses to educate your child, the humble person would open a better school and educate the child of the person who would not educate his. This is how we win them over. Have we not learned that all that could be won by using violence, blood, and death has been gathered by now? We must heal this wasteland.

The great C. S. Lewis defined pride as the most "damnable sin." Regarding pride Lewis said:

> Pride gets no pleasure out of having something, only out of having more of it than the next man.... It is the comparison that makes you proud: the pleasure of being above the rest. Once the element of competition has gone, pride is gone.

The only person you should ever compete with is yourself. Always try to become a better you than you were the day before. Look to GOD as your standard, never man.

GOD has blessed us all with gifts unique only to us. However, many of us walk around with "gift envy." We discount our natural greatness chasing careers, hobbies, and fantasies that lead to suffering and despair. When Black Democrats cry for equality with White America, they are admitting that they hate their Blackness, while White Democrats participating in their movement acknowledge White superiority.

When Conservatives say no set-asides, affirmative action, or laws protecting Blacks are needed because Blacks are awesome, Democrats become apoplectic. White Democrats insist that Blacks cannot succeed as every other minority group has. Black Democrats agree, thus gladly accepting the stamp of inferiority placed upon them by the descendants of these same White Democrats centuries ago.

The opposite of envy is admiration. Where envy lives in the negative hope that people fail, admiration lives in the positive hope that they will succeed and teach you how to succeed. An envious person will see someone in a nice car and hope they wreck. A nurturing person will see a person in a great car, admire it, and ask them how to go about purchasing one.

Eaten up with pride and envy, there are many in the Democrat Party who would like to see America fail because in their pride they are constantly comparing themselves and finding themselves lacking. Then, in their irrational envy, they seek to destroy the very thing that they admire.

We've all seen the picture of the donkey being moved to pull a wagon because a carrot is extended in front of it tied to a stick. It is an illusion. The donkey will never catch the carrot, but the master is getting the donkey to pull his heavy wagon. The donkey is a stupid slave, easily manipulated, easily enticed, and slow to learn. This is why the Democrat Party has it as a mascot. Furthermore, this is how the Democrats will always view their Black constituents.

Why wouldn't they view them as mindless beasts? They've been lying to Black people about returning their forty acres and a mule to them ever since Abraham Lincoln's Democrat successor Andrew Johnson took it from them.

The Democrats are Lucy moving the football, and the Black Democrats are Charlie Brown.

So, if Democrats want to give Black people some money, go ahead and do it. But take note: after attaining the MLK holiday, the taking down of Confederate monuments and flags, the first Black president, and the first Black vice president, Black Democrats are still rioting, still looting, still burning, and still killing each other.

The problem: Democrat leaders have convinced their people to disavow their Christian teachings and believe that their problems can be cured by the hand of man. Democrat leaders have convinced their people that their problems are "without" when Christ tells us they are "within." Jesus has provided us with the remedy. He has demanded that we forgive one another. No amount of money can buy forgiveness or pay for undeserved pain.

Forgiveness cannot be earned, nor should it be wanted or expected. Furthermore, retribution and revenge should never be sought.

Bribery and revenge lead to death. This is the Democrat Party plan. It is an evil plan. It, therefore, reflects them perfectly.

CHAPTER 22:

LIE #21—ONE PARTY RULE IS GOOD

IT IS WIDELY ACCEPTED THAT competition is necessary for improvement. The American system of competition in economic and political affairs has made our country the envy of the world. Nevertheless, like all evil empires, Democrats believe that a one-party socio-communist system is the most desirable.

In this chapter, I will prove three things:

1. Democrat, one-party rule is destructive.
2. The inner city Black community is a perfect example of Democrat one-party rule.
3. One-party rule is suitable only for politicians.

"Potentially, a government is the most dangerous threat to man's rights;
it holds a legal monopoly on the use of physical force against legally disarmed victims."

—Ayn Rand

I am always amazed at the schizophrenia of Black Democrats. They claim that the government is racist, devoid of justice, and oppressive. What is their remedy? More government. Many even prefer the absolute tyranny of one-party rule.

A monopoly is only good when it refers to GOD. The Democrat leaders believe that they are GOD; therefore, I can understand why they see no contradiction here. They are evil; therefore, they are proud of the ghettos, failing schools, crime, drug abuse, poverty, and the prisons that their monopoly has produced. If they weren't proud of it, they'd try to change it. Instead, they will do anything to sustain it.

Monopolies are also supported by fear. Monopolies understand that competition would expose their weaknesses. The strong are never afraid of competition. Muhammad Ali fought all comers. Evander Holyfield followed suit. Insecurity is always suspected when competition is frowned upon.

Furthermore, the wise in any community should demand political and economic competition. Black Democrats funded by White liberals from New York and California are defending their terrible record against Republican candidates who have been abandoned by their party and cannot fight back. It isn't even a contest.

In the Black community, most of the elders do not demand this competition because they are in the pocket of the Democrat Party. These elders seek their own self-interests. The community be damned. And the community has been damned.

The greatest asset of competition is leverage. All your political and economic power derives from leverage. The ability to spend your dollars elsewhere gives you economic power, and the power to cast your vote elsewhere gives you political power. But when you cannot or will not exercise your leverage, you are nothing more than a slave. You are not being loyal or committed; save those emotions for your spouse and GOD. You are being stupid.

There are three things you never let your emotion control: your money, justice, and politics.

Leverage is defined as "to use something to maximum advantage." Once you lose your leverage, you've lost all your power. Leverage is not just having choice; leverage is having the will to exercise choice. The Black community is powerless because the Democrat Party knows there is nothing that the Democrats can do that will cause any portion of that hard-core 90 percent Black vote to walk away from them. When the Black community decided to blindly give all their power to the Democrat Party, like all that have put absolute trust in a single entity other than GOD (the Russians, Cubans, Chinese, and North Koreans), they all became powerless. The results speak for themselves.

There isn't any logical reason why any American should surrender everything and enslave themselves to a political party. It happens in some minor instances to all ethnicities and races. But the Black American's attachment to the Democrat Party borders on insanity. It is un-American. It is immoral. And it is just plain stupid.

After this succinct, lucid, and logical argument, if you still blindly vote for any party, especially the Democrats, you need psychological help.

CHAPTER 23:

LIE #22—ALL BLACK MEN ARE AFRAID

TURN ON YOUR TV TODAY. The media is constantly on the hunt for the story of the fearful Black man. It seems nothing gives them more pleasure than to "dry snitch" or falsely expand the myth that Black men are helpless, can be killed by White men at will, and need the White liberal Democrat to save them.

In this chapter, I will prove four things:

1. All Black men are not afraid.
2. The Democrat Party leadership's power comes from Black fear.
3. If there is nothing for Black people to be afraid of, Democrats will invent it.
4. Fearful Black men verify their inferiority and justify White Democrats' racial superiority complex.

"Fear is the path to the Dark Side."

—Yoda

"For GOD hath not given us the spirit of fear."

—2 Timothy 1:7

Elbert Williams was one of the five charter members of the NAACP in my hometown of Brownsville, Tennessee. He was murdered in 1940 at the age of thirty-one, the first member of the NAACP to die a violent death in their futile quest to end racism. The police had arrested Elbert Williams on June 20, 1940. He was released from the Haywood County jail after his arrest and given to a violent mob of White Democrats from my hometown. They beat him to death and threw his body in the river. His body was found in the Hatchie River on June 23, three days after his arrest. He is buried in an unmarked grave.

Last year, almost eighty years after Elbert William's death, Tennessee began a cold case investigation (when everybody involved is dead). But when it counted, no one was investigated or prosecuted. These White Democrats all walked free.

My home county's history is steeped in all the racist history of the Jim Crow South. Lynchings, murders, and assaults were all conducted by the Democrat Party. Elbert Williams was not a coward. Elbert Williams was not stupid. Elbert Williams was naïve. He thought that all evil men would change when faced with reason and right. Some people will change with truth, but most will not. With those who will not relent, only violence or the threat of violence is sufficient to keep them at bay.

Many Black people suffered throughout the South during these dark times. However, even though I was born on a cotton plantation and my father was a sharecropper at the time of my birth, my siblings and I were protected from the effects of this racism because our father was not a coward and was always armed.

No racist White person ever touched me or called me nigger. At least not to my face. There were and are many Black men like my father; Black men that do not live in fear. You wouldn't know it by reading the newspaper or watching TV.

Embedded in the White supremacist psyche of the Democrat Party is this false belief that all Black men are weak and fear them. The murders of Trayvon Martin, Michael Brown, and George Floyd, while begging for his life, in their minds verify this train of thought. Furthermore, it is magnified when wealthy and powerful Black athletes in the NBA, such as Kareem Abdul-Jabbar and LeBron James, as well as Colin Kaepernick in the NFL, consistently advertise their fear and cowardice all over the world via Twitter, Facebook, Instagram, or anywhere else where they are allowed to cry like schoolyard sissies about how they are oppressed, famous, and adored millionaires.

Three hundred sixty-five times our Holy Bible records the phrase "fear not." One phrase for every day of the year. This is not a coincidence. I grew up during the era of Muhammad Ali, Jim Brown, Doug Williams, John Shaft, and the Black Panthers. Weak, effeminate, and fearful Black men were frowned upon in my home. There existed a masculine Christianity among the men who mentored me.

Today, these strong men still exist but are ignored by the mainstream media. While the fearful are paraded and heralded throughout America and are told to be looked upon as brave, masculinity is defined as toxic. Bravery is being redefined as vigilantism. The Democrats have decided that 2+2=5. And manliness is now defined as cowardice, and cowardice is defined as manly.

Democrats exalt Black people who define beatings, sit-ins, freedom rides, death, envy, hatred, fear, riots, and protest as bravery. They promote the men who have been taught to believe that dying for freedom is honorable, instead of making the person die trying to take your freedom. But they marginalize and leave in the shadows those Black men who not only hold themselves to high standards of honor and responsibility but also demand that others do likewise.

When I think of bravery, I am reminded of a story by historian Barbara Fields during her appearance on Ken Burns's *The Civil War*, regarding a convention of freed Black people in 1863 demanding that Black men be allowed to take part as soldiers for their own liberation during the Civil War. They set out a resolution at the end of their convention that said:

> It is time now for more effective remedies to be thoroughly tried in the shape of warm lead and cold steel duly administered by 100,000 Black Doctors.

When White men almost destroyed New York during the Draft Riots of 1863, refusing to be drafted to bring freedom to Black slaves, Lincoln understood that the Union would lose the war without more men. He put out a call for Black volunteers. Almost 200,000 joined the Union Army. This number constituted 87 percent of all eligible Black men in the North. The South was defeated in less than two years. These free Black men saved America.

When I think of bravery, I am reminded of Alex Turner. Alex Turner was a slave who escaped from his plantation and the cruelty of his Black overseer at the start of the Civil War and joined the First New Jersey Calvary of the Union Army. During the spring of 1863, Turner led his regiment to his old plantation. There he killed his old overseer and liberated his old plantation.

When I think of bravery, I am reminded of this place named Chubbtown. The eight Chubb brothers—John, George, Isaac, Henry, Jacob, William, Thomas, and Nicholas—all free men of color, bought land and built a town in the Confederate States of

America in the state of Georgia. These eight brothers purchased 120 acres of land for $900 in 1964. The settlement grew to include a school, post office, meeting hall, lodge, sawmill, syrup mill, and a casket company. These free Black families farmed the land and were self-sufficient. While General William Sherman burned every Southern town he encountered during the Civil War, the people in Chubbtown were so impressive that he did not touch it, leaving Chubbtown unharmed.

I discovered Chubbtown after noticing the Cleveland Browns' running back, Nick Chubb, during the 2020 NFL season. Most NFL players today are prideful, tattooed, and full of braggadocio. Nick Chubb stood out to me because he had no visible body art. He didn't have a crazy hairstyle and conducted himself quite differently from the rest of the many pampered and frightened young men in the league. In other words, he had an air about him. I researched Mr. Chubb, and when I discovered his heritage, it explained his demeanor.

He was a descendant of free Men. These men were not fearful. They were not victims. The force of these Black men's character was so powerful that even during the times of slavery and the Jim Crow South, racist Democrats were forced to acknowledge their virtue. Black men with the character of the Chubbtown brothers still exist. But 160 later, the mainstream media would prefer to focus on the victims and the crybabies. These large, muscular, oppressed Supermen. Can you imagine how powerful White men must feel when these strong, wealthy, and powerful Black men admit to the world that they fear them?

If you are Black and want to become famous, all you need to do is let it be known that you are afraid of White people, and you need the Democrat Party to come to your rescue. The media will make you a star. After the tragic killing of twenty-year-old Daunte Wright on April 14, 2021, the *Guardian* and other outlets reported George Floyd's brother Philonise Floyd saying,

"The world is traumatized, watching another African American man being slain. Every day I wake up, I never thought that this world could be in so much disorder like it is now." They are hunting Black men. On May 25, 2021, a CNN.com headline attributed to Philonise Floyd read, "If the U.S protects the bald eagle, it can make laws 'to protect people of color.'" His family lawyer, Benjamin Crump, concurred. These Democrats do not understand that most Black men are lions. They are not hunted. They do the hunting.

Sadly, fear is contagious. These fearful Black men have infected Black America with it. Fear is paralyzing, irrational, and defeating. Fear is also not of GOD. Actually, 2 Timothy 1:7 says, "For GOD has not given us a spirit of fear, but of power and of love and a sound mind." Remember, the phrase "fear not" is mentioned in the Bible 365 times, one time for every day in the year.

How can one be a good Christian and also be fearful? You can't. It is impossible. Isn't it ironic that, as Black people drift farther and farther from the word of GOD, Black society becomes more and more dysfunctional and the Democrat Party becomes more and more powerful? It is a paradox. In Revelation 3:15–16, it is said, "I rather you be hot or cold. If you are lukewarm, I spew you out." Can one be monetarily rich and poor at the same time? No. And no one can be afraid and a good Christian.

As I mentioned earlier, Thomas Wolfe stated, "Culture is the arts elevated to a set of beliefs." What art has created the culture of Black America? Hip-hop, gangster rap music, and TV designed to make Black people feel afraid. Movies that I hate like *Mississippi Burning, Selma, 12 Years a Slave*, and the like are cultural cyanide for Black people. They are part of our cultural genocide. Democrats have decided to rewrite our past by excluding the brave Black men who didn't desire any part of this present debacle. This is how Democrats control our future.

I enjoy the old Blaxploitation movies of the late 1960s and early '70s. They depicted the other side of Black America. After the emasculation of the Civil Rights Movement, these movies depicted the other Black men as unafraid and unbowed. The movie *Glory* was great, but it was released twenty-one years ago. Even the movie *Panther*, released in 1995, displayed some Black men as unafraid. But now it seems every film depicts a Black person dying to be loved by White people or are getting their butt kicked by White men.

You wouldn't know it by watching TV or reading public school history textbooks, but all Black people did not support the Civil Rights Movement. In the documentary *Pariah: The Lives and Deaths of Sonny Liston*, when heavyweight champion Sonny Liston was asked why he hadn't participated in the Civil Rights Movement, he responded that he's not going to get involved "if all they're going to do is catch punches."

There were even militant Black organizations that conspired to murder members of prominent civil rights organizations. The Revolutionary Action Movement (RAM) was one such organization. Two of RAM's more notable members were Mutulu Shakur (the stepfather of Tupac Shakur) and Afeni Shakur (the mother to Tupac Shakur). Maxwell Stanford was the leader of RAM, and in 1967, he and sixteen other RAM members were arrested on conspiracy charges for allegedly plotting to assassinate the NAACP's Roy Wilkins and Urban League's Whitney Young. Many members went underground or fled overseas, where some remain. But most of them spent time in prison on these charges.

This story contradicts the Democrat Party lie that the FBI hated civil rights organizations solely because they were Black. If this had been true, the FBI would have stood idly by, watched these Black leaders' assassinations, arrest the members of RAM, and put them in jail forever—thus, declaring victory with clean hands. But instead, the FBI put an end to the plot, saving Wilkins's and Young's lives.

The problem facing the FBI or J. Edgar Hoover was never hatred toward Black citizens. It was the all-legitimate fight against communism and their stated goal of exploiting the Civil Rights Movement to destabilize and ultimately destroy the United States of America. Communists make their home in the Democrat Party. The FBI was given a license to destroy communists in America. This means that the FBI was destroying members of the Democrat Party. Now, Democrats and their friends in the press must convince America that the FBI did nothing good. In an attempt to destroy their reputation, the Democrats must convince America that the FBI was just a racist, rogue organization that hated Blacks.

Democrats really hated the FBI of 1945–1975 because they were the most proficient hunters of communists, racists, and anti-American traitors in history. Ironically, most of those arrested were Democrats. Anyone attempting to change America outside the constitutional process was on the FBI radar. If they were KKK, anti-war, Marxists, Black Panther Marxists, Black Nationalists, or socialists, it did not matter. It is illuminating when one surmises that most of these radicals were members of the Democrat Party. This fact, I'm sure, has added to Democrat hatred of the FBI and J. Edgar Hoover.

Strong, unafraid Black men like my father never depended on the FBI, the police, or civil rights organizations to protect their families. My father did it himself. My brothers and I are like him, and all my friends are like me. We are strong and unafraid. We have no part in this cowardly movement of pride, envy, hate, and disrespect. We believe in strength, forgiveness, admiration, humbleness, and love for all mankind. But we also believe in protecting and defending what we love and own. This is our duty. This is what GOD expects.

So to Supreme Court Justice Clarence Thomas, Congressman Burgess Owens, Senator Tim Scott, Larry Elder, my brothers (Marvin, Robert, Jonathan, Timothy, John, and Ruben), the Hodge twins, C. L. Bryant, James Harris, and Candace Owens: stay strong, represent, and keep telling the truth.

CHAPTER 24:

LIE #23—DEMOCRATS BELIEVE IN SCIENCE

MERRIAM-WEBSTER'S DICTIONARY defines "science" as "the state of knowing: knowledge as distinguished from ignorance or misunderstanding." Democrats advertise that they are a party of science, not a party of ignorance and superstition. But is that really true? In this chapter, I will prove four things:

1. Democrats believe in science when it fits their plans of atheism, murder, and theft.

2. Democrats ignore the science that does not press forward their agenda.

3. To Democrats, science is not an instrument of knowledge but an instrument of control.

4. To Democrats, science is not utilized to build but to destroy.

"This most beautiful system of the sun,
Planets, and comets, could only
proceed from the counsel and dominion
of an intelligent and powerful being."

—Sir Isaac Newton

For the first 200 years of their existence, Democrats attempted to prove that Black people were subhuman and an inferior race through science. They used eugenics, phrenology, apostate religion, and evolution. Indeed, Democrat Supreme Court Chief Justice Roger Taney wrote in the Dred Scott decision:

> On the contrary, they [Blacks] were at the time [of America's founding] considered as a subordinate and inferior class of beings, who had been subjugated by the dominant race, and, whether emancipated or not, yet remained subject to their authority, and had no rights or privileges but such as those who held power and the government might choose to grant them.

The science of the Democrat Party leadership superseded the teachings of Jesus Christ that commanded we love one another and treat each other the way we would like to be treated. Darwinism and science dictate that the strong should overtake the weak and right makes might. There is no place in science for love, mercy, repentance, shame, sacrifice, or regret.

But Democrats Party leadership does not believe in science. They believe in power. Science is wielded as a means to maintain and increase this power. Any science that supports their evil platform, they support. Any science that contradicts their sadist plans, they hastily refute.

We are to believe that after the 1965 Voting Rights Act, 200 years of Democrat Party racism just completely evaporated.

When Democrats claim they believe in science, sometimes they have to pick their poison. Take evolution as an example. When the Democrats were racist against Blacks, they used the science of evolution to justify their racism. Since most atheists were also Darwinist, atheists became some of the largest donors to the Democrat Party. When Democrats could no longer keep Black people from voting, and couldn't let them vote Republican but also had to satisfy the atheist vote, Democrats stopped using evolution to justify racism and started using it to justify atheism. This switch became much easier when Democrats gleefully discovered that they could buy most Black preachers, who in turn made sure that Christian Blacks would support Democrats over GOD and would never leave them under any circumstances.

Today, it is not even mentioned that the theory of evolution was used as a tool of White supremacy. Nevertheless, in a book called *The Timetables of African-American History*, author Sharon Harley wrote:

> Charles Darwin's *On the Origin of Species by Means of Natural Selection* is published; in the work he argues that all species have evolved through a long process of "natural selection" in which species with particular traits reproduce; *this popular but controversial theory is applied socially to oppress people of color and is used to justify Anglo-Saxon domination and imperialism over oppressed people.* [Author's italics]

In an effort to cover the racism behind Darwinism, the "powers that be" have even buried the complete name of the book. The complete name is the book is *On the Origin of Species by Means of Natural Selection, or the Preservation of Favoured*

Races in the Struggle for Life. Who are these "favoured races" of which Darwin speaks?

Nazis believed that these favored nations were Aryan. In the book *From Darwin to Hitler*, author Richard Weikart argues that without Darwin, there would be no Hitler. Dr. Jerry Bergman wrote on November 1, 1999, that "leading Nazis, and early 1900 influential German biologists, revealed in their writings that Darwin's theory and publications had a major influence upon Nazi race policies."

Democrats can't have it both ways. If you believe in evolution, you must believe in both Black inferiority and atheism. The evidence suggests that they do believe in both.

If Democrats believed in science, they would believe these scientific facts:

1. Life begins at conception.
2. Evolution is a theory, not a fact.
3. Freedom and capitalism are superior to tyranny and socialism.
4. Humans cannot control the weather.
5. Abortion is murder.
6. There is no genetic link to homosexuality.
7. The "XX" chromosome = woman. The "XY" chromosome = man.

8. GOD does exist.

9. Animals and man are not equal.

10. Men and women are different.

These are facts. They are absolutely true. Nevertheless, Democrats are so proficient in lying that they may have convinced themselves that their lies are truth.

CHAPTER 25:

LIE #24—THE GOD-HEAD FAMILY IS NO LONGER NEEDED

WHAT IS THE GOD-HEAD family? It is a family that is organized based on the principles relayed in the Holy Bible. Practiced in society for centuries, this structure has been proven to be remarkably successful and the foundation of powerful nations. However, for the past sixty years, this structure has been under constant assault by the Democrat Party. Is the GOD-head family obsolete, or does it still have value?

In this chapter, I will prove four things:

1. The GOD-head family is the original and only true definition of family.

2. The devolution of the GOD-head family is at the heart of every problem in society.

3. Evil people desire to destroy the GOD-head family, therefore controlling the Democrat Party, and are using its power to hasten its destruction.

4. The destruction of the GOD-head family will lead to the destruction of America, which is the goal of the Democrat Party and has been since the issue of the Virginia and Kentucky Resolutions.

"It is from the traditional family that we absorb those universal ideals and principles which are the teaching of Jesus, the bedrock of our religious faith. We are taught the difference between right and wrong, and about the law, just punishment and discipline."

—Kamisese Mara

On March 13, 2013, the Brookings Institution published an article illustrating three actions, if taken, that almost guarantee that a United States citizen will never live in poverty. It says:

> Let politicians, schoolteachers and administrators, community leaders, ministers, and parents drill into children the message that in a free society, they enter adulthood with three major responsibilities: at least finish high school, get a full-time job and wait until age 21 to get married and have children.
>
> Our research shows that of American adults who follow these three simple rules, only about 2 percent are in poverty, and nearly 75 percent have joined the middle class.

With their advocacy of premarital sex, abortion, LGBTQ, religious repression, economic deprivation, mass incarceration, terrible education, and so forth, the Democrat Party leadership has tried everything in their power to ensure that these three things are as difficult as possible

On February 19, 2020, the *Washington Post* reported that in recent years, life expectancy had small annual decreases caused mainly by diseases of despair: drug overdoses, alcoholism, and suicide. It said:

> Flat and modestly declining life expectancy from 2015 to 2017 caused considerable concern among public health experts.... In 2019, life expectancy ticked back up as the number of fatal drug overdose dropped slightly for the first time in 28 years.... "This is a big departure. We haven't seen anything this large since the first half of the 20th century...," said Elizabeth Arias, a health scientist for the NCHS and lead author of the paper....
>
> Furthermore, Black and Latino Americans were hit harder than Whites.... Black Americans lost 2.7 years of life expectance, and Latinos lost 1.9. White life expectancy fell 0.8 years.

For over 2,000 years, it has been argued that the structure of the traditional GOD-head family, consisting of one husband, one wife, and children, was necessary for humankind's survival and prosperity. This assumption has been questioned periodically during those 2,000 years and today generally dismissed by the Democrat Party. Why does a woman need a husband? Why do children need a father? Why do children need a mother? Why do parents need to be married? Why can't people have multiple marriages? "You don't" has been the answer the Democrats have given to the world since the 1960s. These fringe ideas of lunacy have passed out of the concept of theory and have entered into the realm of pure fact. Consequently, the statistics show that America is dying just as the Democrats planned.

Feminist Margaret Drabble said, "Family life itself, that safest, most traditional, most approved of female choices, is not a sanctuary; it is, perpetually, a dangerous place." The anti-family mob consisting of the radical feminist, LGBTQ, atheists, communists, and anarchists honestly believe that the family is dangerous and repressive. If you do not believe this, you should not be a part of the Democrat Party.

On February 21, 2020, W. Bradford Wilcox, professor of sociology at the University of Virginia, wrote for the *Atlantic* magazine, "Children raised in communities with high percentages of single mothers are less likely to move up.... Likewise, communities are stronger and safer when they include lots of committed married couples."

On November 2, 2015, the *Illinois Review* reported on a study by the Brookings Institution and Princeton University that concluded: "Most scholars now agree that children raised by two biological parents in a stable marriage do better than children in other family forms across a wide range of outcomes." It also reported that the *Washington Post* stated, "On most economic indicators, the share of parents who are married in a state is a better predictor of that state's economic health than the racial composition and educational attainment of the state's residents."

These statistics are all well known to Democrats. The fact that Democrats refuse to change direction proves that they are happy with this current arrangement. The destruction of the Black family by the Democrat Party welfare system has led to the dysfunction and dystopia in the inner cities and in the majority Black districts. The more dysfunction Democrats can inflict on the

GOD-head family, the more power Democrats wield. Democrat power comes through pain. The more pain they cause, the more power they wield.

Democrat leadership believes that they are wiser than GOD. They have the nerve to question His commandments. Why do what GOD says? Because GOD said it. That settles it. When Job had the nerve to question GOD about Job's suffering, GOD answered him in a whirlwind and said, "Who is this that darkens counsel by words without knowledge? Gird up your loins like a man, I will question you, and you shall declare to me."

CHAPTER 26:

LIE #25—BLACK PEOPLE WERE NOT AND ARE NOT FREE

THE CONCEPT OF FREEDOM has been debated since the Garden of Eden. The common refrain of "we want our freedom" has emanated from the Black community since 1619. Ironically, today this call for "Black freedom" is magnified by the Black communities' primary enslaver, the Democrat Party. There are an American concept of freedom and a Democrat Party concept of freedom. The American concept of freedom has changed the world for the better. The Democrat Party concept has attempted to enslave it. What is this American concept of freedom? And why has the Democrat Party convinced Black Americans that they do not possess it?

In this chapter, I will prove eight things:

1. Freedom is a gift from GOD.

2. Government cannot bestow freedom.

3. Enslavement is not physical. It is a frame of mind where one refuses to take responsibility for one's

choices and blames others.

4. Freedom is an absolute. Coercion is a lie. Right or wrong, negatively or positively, your choices will affect your life. Therein lies your power.

5. What is done to you does not affect your freedom. How you respond to it does.

6. Every person ever born, including Black people, were born free.

7. Those who exclaim that they are not free and need government permission before they can exercise their freedom have fallen for the Democrat Party lie.

8. Convincing every American to choose slavery is the primary goal of the Democrat Party.

"What state all men are naturally in, and that is, a state of perfect freedom to order their actions, and dispose of their possessions and persons, as they see fit…without asking leave, or depending upon the will of any other man."

—John Locke, 1689

"So, if the Son set you free, you will be free indeed."

—John 8:36

"The truth will make you free."

—John 8:32

"For we were called to freedom, brothers. Only do not use freedom as an opportunity for the Flesh, but through love, serve one another."

—Galatians 5:13

A slave mind and an absolute belief in the power of government over GOD are necessities before a person can gain the title of Black leader in the Democrat Party. The Black preachers are the caretakers of the spiritual education of Black children. These preachers should consistently remind Black people that their freedom is a gift from GOD. Instead, they obey their White Democrat masters by consistently attributing the freedom of Black people to government. Sadly, Blacks are the only ethnic group in America that do not attribute their freedom to GOD. Consequently, Blacks as an ethnic group consistently remain at the bottom of every socioeconomic statistic in the Western world.

Black academics are no better. In his PBS documentary called *The Black Church*, Black Harvard professor Henry Louis "Skip" Gates Jr. stated, "On New Year's Eve 1862, northern black congregations held watch night services, desperately praying, singing, anxiously awaiting the hour of freedom.... With Lincoln's signature on New Year's Day, the Emancipation Proclamation stated that "all persons held as slaves in the rebel states shall be henceforward and forever free."

Reginald F. Hildebrand of Durham Technical Community College emotionally said of the Emancipation Proclamation, "This is a confirmation that their prayers have been answered... free, free, free."

During the March on Washington, Dr. Martin Luther King Jr. attributed Black freedom to government documents and laws. King said:

> When the architects of our republic wrote the magnificent words of the Constitution and the Declaration of Independence, they were signing a promissory note to which every American was to fall heir. This note was a promise that all men, yes, black men as well as white men, would be guaranteed the inalienable rights of life, liberty, and the pursuit of happiness.

Maybe someone should have reminded the Ivy League–educated, good reverend-doctor that unalienable rights do not come from, nor can be guaranteed by, man or government. They come from GOD and are guaranteed and protected by GOD and the individual. Government and man are usually the violators of these rights. For these reasons, government should remain small and weak while the individual and his reverence for his GOD must remain paramount.

The Jews are successful because their history records that they chose to credit their freedom to GOD: they owe GOD their lives and obedience. Black history records that most Black Americans credit their freedom to a government or a man (Abe Lincoln, Martin Luther King Jr., John F. Kennedy): Blacks, therefore, have chosen to credit their lives and obedience to the government and have continuously suffered for this mistake.

What if your father gave you a gift of $10 million? To help secure this gift and keep it safe, you deposit it in a bank for safety. Do you thank your father for that money, or do you thank the bank? Only a fool would give the bank credit for that gift. If you decided to credit the bank and not your father, it would be understandable that your father would be offended.

Take this exact scenario and apply it to your freedom. GOD, your father, has given you the priceless gift of freedom. You install a government to assist you in protecting that freedom. But instead of thanking GOD for granting you this gift, you thank the government. You even believe that the government has the right and power to take, limit, or destroy this gift from GOD at will. You, therefore, allow it to control this gift and thereby control you. You've placed GOD under government. If you are a fool in the first scenario, you are also a fool here.

Democrats have spread this lie regarding freedom for generations. Some Americans, but most Black Americans, have accepted it as an absolute. Whenever I hear that Abraham Lincoln freed the slaves, I am reminded of this misguided line of thinking. Abraham Lincoln deserves all the credit due to him for issuing the Emancipation Proclamation and for shepherding the Thirteenth Amendment through the arduous confirmation process. Nevertheless, man's freedom is a gift from GOD, not man or his government. This freedom is irreversible, irrevocable, and nontransferable. Therefore, it is a metaphysical fact that these government documents did not free one slave. When a man is full of fear, envy, and pride, not even the great Abraham Lincoln could convince him to leave his master's plantation. These great documents only changed the federal and state government's relationship from assisting in the indentured servitude of its Black citizens to supporting the freedom of them. Before and after these documents, a slave still followed orders, and a free man still walked wherever he pleased.

However, like GOD'S salvation, GOD'S freedom must be accepted. And many Black Americans refused to accept it then and refuse to accept it now. The Democrat Party remains their master. In the mind of a slave, his master must be obeyed. They must attribute to him everything that comes to their life, the good and the bad. Therefore, it is not strange that the Black Democrat must attribute his slavery to his White master and his freedom to Abraham Lincoln. But the two primary players in this saga, him and GOD, are not given any blame or credit.

Understand this: freedom requires action. If one does not accept the responsibility, one then must experience the social, economic, and spiritual humiliation that accompanies cowardice.

Like anything else of value, your freedom will not stay unclaimed. You must proclaim yourself "free," or someone else will claim it and enslave you. Whether you like it or not, you are the caretaker of your freedom. You decide when and how to exercise this freedom. If you admit that you are born free today, you must also admit that your ancestors were born free 220 years ago. You can only be enslaved with your permission. And like our ancestors before 1865, most Black Americans today still allow themselves to be enslaved by the Democrat Party.

On August 14, 1862, Abraham Lincoln invited a delegation of Black clergy to the White House to discuss the resettlement of Black slaves in a place where they would be free of the racism and the hatred of their former White Democrat masters.

Like Democrat Andrew Jackson had forced the resettlement of Indians between 1830 and 1850, conservative Republican Abraham Lincoln could have forced this resettlement upon the newly emancipated Black slaves. But believing in freedom, he gave them a choice, and they decided to stay in the South with their former masters. I am glad they chose to stay in America. Nevertheless, I lose patience with these Black nationalists, Black power militants, Black victims, and Blacks in general who have pardoned the questionable decision of their ancestors, refusing Black independence, and accepting second-class citizenship in America, while concurrently placing blame on the United States and perpetually complaining about their present condition.

Black Americans could have conducted a revolution against their White oppressors. Revolutions were conducted in Haiti against the French, the United States against Great Britain, and South America and Cuba against Spain. But most Black Americans who shunned revolution chose to remain American citizens and naturally gravitated to their home in the Democrat Party, where their traditional position of submission, fear, envy, and pride waited for them.

To bestow upon any man or government the veneration and appreciation for your freedom is an affront to GOD and limits your ability to serve Him and do His will.

The Thirteenth Amendment only guaranteed that evil men could no longer use government power to force people to work for nothing; that freed slaves could now utilize the power of government to assist them in maintaining their freedom. The Thirteenth Amendment reads:

> Neither Slavery nor involuntary servitude, except as a punishment for crime whereof the party shall have been duly convicted, shall exist within the United States, or any place subject to their jurisdiction.

The Thirteenth Amendment is not the Emancipation Proclamation. The Emancipation Proclamation was a war necessity written by Lincoln alone to defeat an enemy. The Thirteenth Amendment was added to the Constitution. It was reviewed and microscopically and forensically investigated by the greatest freedom philosophers in the halls of Congress and academia of the day. These great minds understood that men and governments could not bestow freedom, only GOD. For this reason, freedom is never mentioned in the Thirteenth Amendment. The government cannot bestow it, but it can violate and abridge it. If a bank confiscates your funds, are they not still your funds? Of course, they are. The bank is now a thief. Should you celebrate the thief when the thief returns to you the gift given to you by your father? No. You never trust the thief again.

Democrats have convinced too many Americans that their freedom was bestowed upon them by government, and they must rely on government for that freedom and everything it entails. They must do this. With this lie of lies, they maintain control. How could the Democrats have controlled the slave without first convincing them that they could not be free without their permission?

Nevertheless, some slaves knew in their hearts that they were not owned by another man and did not need, or want, his permission to exercise his freedom. Two of the most famous were Harriet Tubman and Fredrick Douglass. And then there were those slaves, over 90 percent, who not only believed that they were slaves but passed this belief down to their children even to this generation.

The Black community's civil rights leaders, preachers, and politicians maintain this lie. To satisfy their masters, slave-minded Black Americans consistently march, loot, and cry that they want freedom. It's like having $1 million in the bank but not using it because you believe the bank controls it. All of them who march and loot are too ignorant to understand that they already possess their freedom but are too afraid to exercise it.

Restating the quote from William Faulkner, "The past is never dead. It's not even past." The slave trade still exists. There is a tremendous amount of profit connected to it. The greatest difference, sadly, is that the slaves pre-1865 admitted they were slaves. The house Negroes knew they were house Negroes, and the master knew that they were masters. Today's Blacks will say that they are not free but will deny that they are slaves, will not admit they have masters, and believe the abolitionists are actually the house Negroes.

Who benefits from this new slave trade? The Democrat Party.

Conservatives have always believed in freedom. We believe that Jesus Christ made us free. John 8:36 reads, "If the Son, therefore, shall make you free, ye shall be free indeed." We do not believe in stress, envy, or hatred. I do not stand with the people who looted the Capitol on January 6, 2020. That was not a Christian act. It was not a conservative act. It was stupid, illegal, and wrong. We believe Philippians 4:6, "The peace of God, which surpasses all understanding, will guard your hearts and minds in Christ Jesus." We do not covet our neighbor's possessions and then, after finding ourselves wanting, use government as a tool to rob them.

Democrats are so good at lying that they have convinced their followers to believe that with a snap of their fingers, government has the power to make them equal with the people they most admire; the government has the power to make them rich; the government has the power to make them free. Never understanding that to wish for such things is an admission to a severe inferiority complex. The Democrats have been very proficient at cultivating this sense of inferiority among its members.

But here's the good news. Because you are free, you can control every aspect of your life. You can choose. "I call heaven and earth to record this day against you, that I have set before you life and death, blessing and cursing: Therefore, *CHOOSE* life, that both thou and thy seed may live." You are free. You are free to choose life. Life does not come from following man. Life comes from following the gospel of Jesus Christ. And that is GOOD NEWS!

EPILOGUE:

THE SLAUGHTERHOUSE

AS A CHILD ATTENDING CHURCH on Sunday morning in Haywood County, Tennessee, I recall experiencing a cavalcade of emotions whenever the Black preacher delivered a sermon explaining how GOD had cursed me. In his sermons, he would mention "the Curse of Ham," as recorded in Genesis 9:20–27. He would say the curse had turned African skin dark. The preacher continued by saying GOD had stamped my family, me, and all Black people with a badge of inferiority and damned us to a life in service to our "superior": the White man. To not obey would be a sin.

For years I dealt with this. It reiterated time and time again by those well-meaning but ignorant Black people in my community looking for a reason besides their own wretchedness to justify their plight in life. However, when I learned to read, I discovered that this curse was a lie.

It was a devious lie devised centuries earlier by Europeans to justify the African transatlantic slave trade and used by Democrat Party slaveholders to justify their inhumane treatment of Blacks. These slaveholders then forced this lie upon their children, imbuing them with a demonic mentality capable of the most horrific atrocities known to man. Worse yet, these Democrats slaveholders trained the Black preacher to impart this lie into the mind and heart of the slave, who then grafted it into the DNA of their descendants. This lie still haunts Black people and all of America to this very day, if not in words, definitely in deeds.

For the formative years of my life, I believed that GOD had cursed me and everyone who looked like me. I was a dark-skinned Black boy, and the darker you were, the more you were cursed. GOD gave me the grace to journey out of this morass. Nevertheless, when I realized that these people would even lie about the contents of the Holy Bible to maintain their control, I understood that their evil had no boundary. Since then, most of the people who seek to maintain control over me have no credibility. But others are still trapped. They will deny it, of course. However, their actions betray them.

How do the Democrats convince people to destroy themselves? They first must persuade them to hate themselves. They will then destroy not only themselves but everyone who resembles them. To do that, they must lie to them as they lied to me.

The lie is wrapped in bells, whistles, parades, and loudness. The liars convey absolute authority by falsely evoking the word of GOD along with the trappings of wealth, access, and prestige. The lie is a drug that makes you numb to the damage you're doing to yourself and blind to the destruction you force on others. Their goal is to lead you peacefully into the "Slaughterhouse."

In my mind, I have seen this Slaughterhouse. It is a place designed to destroy your soul, mind, and body. I've seen the dead bodies of millions of babies, Black slaves, poor Whites, sharecroppers, and Union soldiers murdered there. I've seen the destroyed lives of millions of molested, exploited, and abused children; prison inmates; welfare mothers; inner city children; drug addicts; AIDS patients; and transgender men and women; along with Christians in holding cages waiting for slaughter.

In the midst of the Slaughterhouse sits a giant reaper that separates the victims so they can be consumed by a Devourer. Each Devourer has a different appetite. Some desire children to molest or torture. Others prefer the slave to rape and oppress. Most, like ancient Romans in the Coliseum, want only to witness bloody death. This Slaughterhouse has operated in all types of weather, night and day, for over 220 years, servicing these Devourers' devious appetites and lusts.

In my mind I ask, *How do I stop the operators of this Slaughterhouse*? Do I reason with them by asking them to change their ways? Do I negotiate for its closure? Do I present it with a cease-and-desist order?

No. This place is evil. There is no negotiation with Evil.

Then what do I do to a house that taught a race of people and a child that GOD has cursed them? A house painted in the blood of unborn children; a house built on a foundation of murder and lies; a house where Satan lays his head—this wretched Slaughterhouse. What do I do to stop it?

I BLOW IT UP!

ACKNOWLEDGMENTS

David Limbaugh Esq.
Sean Hannity
AJ Rice
Kip Smith
Michele Odom
Judy Kent
David Almasi
My daughters

ABOUT THE AUTHOR

VINCE EVERETT ELLISON was born on a cotton plantation in Haywood County, Tennessee. His parents at that time were sharecroppers. Through hard work and a belief in Jesus Christ, his parents pulled him and his seven siblings out of poverty. His family started the Ellison Family Gospel singing group, where Vince sang and played multiple instruments as a child and young adult. Vince worked for five years as a Correctional Officer at the Medium/Maximum Kirkland Correctional Institution in Columbia, SC. Afterward, Vince worked in the nonprofit arena.

In 2000, Vince received the Republican Party nomination for the South Carolina 6th Congressional District. In 2019, Vince wrote *The Iron Triangle: Inside the Liberal Democrat Plan to Use Race to Divide Christians and America in their Quest for Power and How We Can Defeat Them*, which became an Amazon #1 bestseller. He has appeared numerous times on *Hannity, The Laura Ingraham Show*, Newsmax, OAN, *The Joe Pags Show, The Brian Kilmeade Show, The Howie Carr Show*, and many other radio and television programs.

Vince is a member of Project 21 and has written numerous articles for *American Greatness* magazine, Bizpacreview.com, and other publications.

Made in the USA
Columbia, SC
08 July 2024

f03517c2-ee42-4fcb-ac18-8e0d8aa95ea6R01